Real Life Prepper

Real Life Prepper

By Frank Cohee

First Edition
Intelligent Arms, LLC
Birmingham, AL
March 2014

ISBN: 0615985084
ISBN-13: 978-0-615-98508-4

DEDICATION

Real Life Prepper is dedicated to God and to RLP's family. Support and understanding are critical to being able to work in a creative manner. I pray that *Real Life Prepper* will help someone to prepare in this life. However, preparation for the next life and a relationship with our Savior, Jesus, is a matter of the heart and soul and is much more important.

DISCLAIMER

Yes, RLP is right more than he is wrong. But please pay attention to the following. It will be repeated elsewhere. What you see here are RLP's opinions and thoughts and recommendations. RLP is not an accountant, an attorney, a medical professional, a financial advisor, or even a registered engineer. RLP's opinions, recommendations, and thoughts are offered to you with the best of intentions but any actions you take are based on your personal evaluation of those ideas. RLP has not solicited any compensation from any vendor of any product discussed in *Real Life Prepper*. I cannot be held legally responsible for any actions that you take.

ACKNOWLEDGMENTS

RLP would like to acknowledge MrsRLP and our two fine sons for their support in this endeavor, particularly in the last three months of completing Real Life Prepper. The rest of the extended RLP family, Faith Presbyterian Church members, and co-workers have also given much support. Thank you from the bottom of my heart.

TABLE OF CONTENTS

INTRODUCTION

Welcome to the world of preparation (sometimes called "prepping"). Folks who have an interest in prepping are called preppers. For some folks, this is just a logical continuation or only a slight modification of their lifestyle. Many of us were Boy Scouts or Girl Scouts. Be prepared, they said. And so we try to be. For other folks, this can be a way of life. In fact, prepping can be all consuming.

We are told not to live in a spirit of fear. But we are also told to take care of ourselves and our families. Regardless of your political leanings, this book may be of some value to you. A hurricane, a tornado, a drought, or a loss of job is no respecter of your political affiliation. Rather than focusing on the reasons for an event that exercises your preparations, we want to spend more time figuring out how to survive, or even thrive when we are faced by some disaster, seen or unforeseen. If you are a new prepper, some may classify you as a sheep. You may want to proceed directly to the "How to Start" chapter. When there are wolves out there, you do not want to be a sheep.

Whether you are personally experiencing a general sense of malaise, or you think you can clearly see the handwriting on the wall, you have seen some signs that things are changing. This book is written to help keep you from being negatively impacted by the changes. Even if you do not see any fundamental changes, you can see history. Large events such as hurricane Katrina, the terrorist attacks on the World Trade Center, or the typhoon in the Philippines still occur with or without our foresight or permission. You owe it to yourself and to your family to prepare.

Real Life Prepper is designed to help you get started on your journey. This is not a guide to a final destination. RLP will make concrete product and action suggestions but that does not mean you have to follow those suggestions. They may not be "best in class" or the best choice for you, but they work and they will help point you to in the right direction. RLP has not solicited any compensation from any vendor of any product discussed in *Real Life Prepper*.

So what the heck is a "real life prepper?" My definition is simply someone who has an interest in being prepared for the events we may face in our lives while continuing to live out their life in as normal a fashion as possible. I will not attempt to define "normal."

Real Life Prepper is written to address the needs of the real life prepper. There are many "doom and gloom" books out there, some that will be discussed in this book. I personally enjoy authors such as James Wesley Rawles and have learned a lot from both his fiction and non-fiction works. Books like *A Failure of Civility* and *Society Ending Events: The First 180 Days* are also extremely useful. But what do we do if we do not face a total collapse of society and no horde of mutant ninja zombie bikers tries to attack us at every turn? I am in no way guaranteeing that society will not collapse. Nor am I guaranteeing that the golden horde will not swarm over your peaceful home to steal all of your food. *Real Life Prepper* will give you the information you need to get started and help you move in the right direction. We stress a common sense approach to prepping. Where you go from there is up to you.

Real Life Prepper is primarily a non-fiction work. There are stories, both real life stories and created scenarios that develop perspective and hopefully communicate key concepts in a better way than a list of facts alone might do. One long story you will be presented with is "A Tale of Two Cities." This story can actually be used as an individual, family, or group exercise. After you read about Sherry and Pepper, there is a list of questions and then some answers. Another longer story is "Real Money: A Fable." Only the characters are fictional. This story sets the stage for financial preparations.

The companion website is designed to be a resource for this book. You can key in an address (URL) for a resource cited in the book, or you can go to the website http://www.reallifeprepper.com and click on the associated link in the document [A000] *Real Life Prepper* Links and Aides to download resources. For example, [A001] Two Cities Exercise and [A002] Two Cities Answers for "A Tale of Two Cities" are available on the website. These are the kinds of resources you may want to download for use in a group or family exercise. A dynamic website will allow us to keep links up-to-date where possible when they change. Most internet links in the book have a link ID followed by the actual link (clickable if you are reading the electronic version). Here is an example that takes you to the Real Life Prepper website: [L001] http://www.reallifeprepper.com. Other aides such as forms and templates may also be downloadable from the website.

Guide to the Book

This is a practical, not a theoretical, guide to preparation for disaster and subsequent survival. It is designed to address most topics in a very broad fashion. In addition, some topics are addressed in a very deep and technical fashion where RLP believes that adds value to your journey. You can learn from it now and you can also save it to refer to later. The internet may not be available when you most need it for reference. However, most cited links in this manual have associated codes. The code refers to a "link guide" on Reallifepepper.com where you may go to get an updated link (if it is available).

The manual is organized by general groupings of common topics. They were partially inspired by the rumored 2013 Federal Government grid outage desktop exercise and associated National Geographic Channel documentary entitled, "American Blackout." Each general group of common topics can be treated as a category and has sub-topics. Of course, there is a certain amount of unavoidable overlap. For instance, flashlight batteries may be discussed in the Energy and Power as well as the lighting category.

Since this a practical guide, it may come off dry at times. Therefore, we have interspersed facts with experiences and even an occasional story that helps solidify a point.

Now for some legal mumbo-jumbo. I am not an attorney, a physician, an accountant, or a psychologist. *Real Life Prepper* does not contain any official legal, medical, or accounting advice. I am just a man; you can call me RLP, crying out in the wilderness. If you try anything out that I talk about here, I am not liable. You are on your own.

Any self-respecting prepper book must have at least a little doom and gloom. So here is our gratuitous contribution. But let's work our way up to it.

Why Prepare?

This question has been asked a million times in

a million different ways. It has also been answered in more than a million different ways. What you may want to do is have some sort of answer to the question, "**Why you prepare?**" Notice I did not say a complete or final answer. There will never be a complete or final answer and the answer for you may not be the same as someone else's answer while both may be correct. Fundamentally, all answers will point back to what we mentioned earlier. We need to take care of ourselves, our families, and potentially others. Another related question (which is where the doom and gloom comes in) is, "**What are you preparing for?**" For instance, if you think it might rain, you might prepare by wearing a raincoat or bringing an umbrella. If you think it might be sunny, you might prepare by wearing a hat or bringing sunglasses.

Most of us want to be left alone to live our lives. For the most part, we want to be able to protect our lives, our liberty, and our pursuit of happiness. Many things can happen that threaten our lives, our liberty, and our pursuit of happiness. Those things can be minor or they can be major. A worse scenario involves multiple or unforeseen threats. Anything that is a viable threat to our lives, liberty, or pursuit of happiness should be at least evaluated and some determination made as to what action you are going to take to mitigate that threat.

Every day events can threaten us or our families. There is no doom or gloom necessary for a threat to materialize and impact us in a negative fashion. You can cut your finger and need a band aid. You can run out of gas. The power can go out at your house. You can lose your wallet. In the spirit of the Boy Scouts, you need to be prepared for these types of events. Preparation for these events is the start of being a *Real Life Prepper*.

It is not unusual for a normal family to only have two or three days' worth of food in their house.

Many families on a trip routinely drive their car until the gas gauge reads empty, and then they fill up at the readily available gas station. Younger folks are particularly susceptible to relying on the government or someone else to bail them out if necessary. Part of that is based on the ubiquity of technology and the bountiful society we are blessed to live in. Many folks say we are only nine meals away from a revolution.

I took one of my employees on a business trip to Texas. This is a real story but I will change his name so he does not sue me. I was prepared for Bob even though he was not prepared for himself. After work, we went to the Salt Lick, a fine Texas barbeque place, for dinner. The Salt Lick takes no checks (which Bob does not use anyway), credit cards, or debit cards. This is a cash only place, honey. Bob attempted to use his well-worn debit card to no avail. As he contemplated having to do the dishes for his supper, I was able to bail him out because I am a *Real Life Prepper*. If Bob had simply carried a little emergency cash, his boss would not have had to bail him out.

Not so common events can also impact you negatively. A home invasion would probably not be in your best interest. A hurricane like Katrina could mess up more than just your day. You could lose your job for a few months and we all know that your children are used to eating.

And for the doom and gloom aficionados, something catastrophic, but not beyond the realm of possibility, could take you out for good. A terrorist attack could shut down the city where you work. An EMP blast over your state could render every electrical device you work with totally useless. Hyper-inflation could wipe out your life savings.

If you are not concerned at all, you are suffering from normalcy bias or you are delusional. If your imagination is now active, you are fairly normal. If you are really scared, you need to stop and take a breath. Remember, this is not *Doomsday Preppers* stuff. We are encouraging reasonable, logical, real life preparations that will at least get you started in the right direction. Still, with so many possibilities, there must be a way to determine what to prepare for. Knowing <u>what</u> to prepare for helps you to know <u>how</u> to prepare.

Prioritizing Disasters

Okay, let's admit it. A large meteor strike on my house while I am asleep would probably leave a mark. Am I prepared for that? Should I prepare for that?

There has to be a way to prioritize disasters so that you might apply the appropriate amount of preparation resources in the right place. This prioritizing system would have to blend subjective ideas with objective analysis and allow us to quantify some thoughts. In addition, it should clearly represent the problem, perhaps in a graphical format.

Here is one such system I developed called the "The Intelligent Graphical Rating System," or TIGRS. Either done by hand or through an Excel spreadsheet, TIGRS requires only two inputs. Each input is based on a simple rating scale with 1 being the lowest and 9 being the highest. The first input is the impact. The second input is the probability. These ratings are subjective.

For those of you who may not be able to see the graph in color, here is an explanation. The size of the three regions on the graph are not as important as the general idea of what each region means. The region in the upper right-hand corner of the graph is red and indicates danger. You probably want to pay attention to any threat that is located in the red region. The middle band is yellow and represents caution. You may or may not take any action for threats that plot here. The region in the bottom left-hand corner is green and represents relative safety. These threats are probably not going to be addressed.

Let me demonstrate one threat as an example. I will call this threat or event, "A." A large meteor strike on my house has an impact of 9. In my subjective opinion, this would be bad. For you, it might have a lesser impact. The probability of a large meteor strike on my house in my subjective opinion is very low. I give it a 1. For you, it might be higher. After this analysis, plot the PROBABLITY on the abscissa (X-axis) and the IMPACT on the ordinate (Y-axis). Note where I placed the "A" on the picture. It is in the yellow zone. I made the decision to not worry about, or prepare, for it.

On the other hand, another event to consider is a tornado, threat/event "B." A tornado has an impact of 7, once again in my subjective opinion. The probability of a tornado striking my house (at least in this example) is a 6. Note where I placed event "B" on the picture. It is in the red zone and I will prepare for it.

TIGRS SAMPLE

IMPACT			1	2	3	4	5	6	7	8	9
	High	9	A								
	High	8									
		7					B				
	Med	6									
	Med	5									
		4									
	Low	3									
	Low	2									
		1									
TIGRS			1	2	3	4	5	6	7	8	9
			Low	Low	Low	Med	Med	Med	High	High	High
			PROBABILITY								

RLP believes that TIGRS can help you filter through some of the noise that bombards us every day. Of course, one needs to exercise some common sense and not plot every possible issue. A [A003] TIGRS Spreadsheet template can be downloaded from the companion website.

After you have filtered through the noise and determined what threats you need to address, it is time to start looking specifically at different aspects of your preparations. Subsequent chapters will assist you in exploring some of these different aspects. But you might ask yourself if there are any transcendent needs. As you move about doing your everyday things in your everyday life, there are everyday rules and everyday laws that must be followed. The law of gravity is one such law. The rule of three is one of the everyday rules that is not really a hard and fast rule but rather a guideline and principle.

The Rule of Three

If you want to kill some time, search on the internet for the "Rule of Three." Here we will address the rule of three in regards to survival. There is even a website dedicated to the rule of three for survival. Check out [L002] http://www.ruleof3survival.com/ . Funny that the "rule of three" has four rules!

Known throughout the prepper universe, the rule of three for survival applies whether you like it or not and whether you pay attention to it or not. It pays attention to you. It is a helpful way to prioritize your survival tasks and perhaps might guide you in some of your preparations.

In an extreme situation,

- You cannot survive for more than three (3) minutes without **air**.
- You cannot survive for more than three (3) hours without **shelter**.
- You cannot survive for more than three (3) days without **water**.
- You cannot survive for more than three (3) weeks without **food**.

Clearly there are exceptions to the rule. There is no finer place to be than in north Alabama in September. You can easily survive more than three hours outside with no shelter. But north Alabama in September is not an extreme situation. Try spending three hours outside in northern New Jersey in January wearing only shorts and a T-shirt. Hey, I have been there, done that, and I have the T-shirt.

Guiding Thoughts

When you start to realize the fragile situation we are all in, and start to prepare, and maybe even get the prepper bug, you will run into certain difficulties. You will want to buy stuff. Gadgets are cool. You will feel naked without buckets of beans. You will feel behind the "real" preppers. Your spouse will resist. Your friends will make fun of you. You will run out of money. Rest assured you have taken a right first step in reading *Real Life Prepper*. This should be required reading for anyone who has a brain. You should start out becoming a *Real Life Prepper*, not a *Doomsday Prepper*. Where you go from being a *Real Life Prepper* is up to you. Think of this as a Prepping 101 course.

There are many proven strategies laid out in *Real Life Prepper*. Proven and tried techniques and products are offered for your consideration. They may not be the best that are out there or even the best for you. But they have been tried and they work. Transcendent to everything here is to help make you a *Real Life Prepper*, a person who has approached preparation in an intelligent manner.

Two is One, One is None
This is a fundamental principle but not a rule of law. What this means is that if you only have one gadget, it stands a good chance of failing when you need it most. If you have only way to clean water, you will probably end up with no clean water. If you have only one flashlight, you will end up in the dark. This is where common sense and money come in. Does it really make sense for you to buy two houses just because one might burn down? Or does it make sense to buy more than one fire extinguisher?

Try What You Buy
This is another fundamental principle, not a rule of law. If you buy the best available dehydrator and have never used it, do not expect to turn out perfect jerky when your refrigerator fails. If you buy a recommended generator and have not practiced starting it and using it, do not be surprised when you cannot get electricity to your refrigerator when the ice storm takes out your

power lines. If you buy 200 pounds of wheat and do not know what to do with it, do not be surprised when your gluten-free wife looks at you with incredulity and your children look at you and the seeds in their breakfast bowl with disgust when the grocery stores cannot open.

Store What You Eat, Eat What You Store

There is no reason for MrsRLP to buy canned beets for long-term storage. I am not eating them now and I will not eat them later. It is a myth that everyone will eat anything when they are hungry enough. Young children and older folks have been known to starve to death rather than eat something that is not familiar or palatable to them. You need to practice. If you store wheat, you should introduce that into your regular meals. How will you grind it? What will you do with it after you grind it? What will you do with all of those beans? Do you know how to turn hard, dried beans into regular food? Are there members of your family that do not tolerate beans well?

Rotate, Rotate, and Rotate

Devise a method to rotate almost everything you purchase. Batteries expire. Peanut butter expires. Band aids expire. Aspirin expires. Gasoline expires. Remember "First In, First Out" or FIFO. Bullets do not expire. Toilet paper does not expire.

Skills Are Better Than Stuff

If you take a first aid course, no one can really take that away from you. If you just buy a first aid kit, many things can happen. The first aid kit can be stolen or burned up in a fire. The first aid kit may not be with you when you need to actually use it. You may reach into the first aid kit and find the adhesive on the band aids gave up their stickiness two years ago. You certainly will not know how to use everything in an extensive first aid kit without some training, and it will be too late to read that tiny print book when you need it. Would you rather own one gun that you know how to operate well or a safe full of guns that you do not even know how to load? With the proper training, you can safely load, operate, and clean a neighbor's gun that you might have to borrow.

"It was the best of times, it was the worst of times, it was the age of wisdom, it was the age of foolishness, it was the epoch of belief, it was the epoch of incredulity, it was the season of Light, it was the season of Darkness, it was the spring of hope, it was the winter of despair, we had everything before us, we had nothing before us, we were all going direct to Heaven, we were all going direct the other way" – Charles Dickens

A TALE OF TWO CITIES

It was November 10, just after midnight, and GRIDEX II was just about to end. Murphy had been working for the North American Electric Reliability Corporation (NERC) for almost ten years. But he was tired. This morning, it was his job to order a simulated shutdown of some Duke Energy power plants for protection of the SERC grid. What he did not know was that a logging truck had left western Tennessee early the previous day and had just entered Western Virginia. The driver was also tired.

Murphy's garbled instructions reached the Duke Energy dispatcher about an hour before the truck driver pulled his rig over to the side of the road to catch some sleep. The truck driver crawled into the back of his sleeper cab and started snoring about the same time the Senior Reactor Operator at Oconee Nuclear Station began his shutdown. Shortly afterwards, the tie-down on the logging truck failed and the logs tumbled off the truck, hitting the base of the nearby electrical transmission tower. The hit was enough to trip the large high-voltage breaker and electrical energy stopped flowing from the ReliabilityFirst Corporation (RFC) region into the Southeastern Reliability Electric Council (SERC) region. The high-voltage breaker immediately reset itself and the resultant grid surge caused the

Oconee Nuclear Station to automatically fail to an emergency shutdown. Three major transformers simultaneously arced and much of the South East was going to be dark for at least a week.

Sherry (the sheep) woke up with the sun streaming into her bedroom.

Something is not right; I usually have to leave before the sun rises.

A quick glance over at the digital display alarm clock reveals… nothing. An already completely booked day suddenly becomes more burdensome. She was supposed to get gas in the car on the way to work since it is running on fumes.

Now I am going to be late for work even without having to stop. But I will not make it without stopping for gas. I will just have to reschedule my first meeting. And I will have to eat a quick breakfast, no oatmeal for me today.

After climbing out of bed, she checks her watch on the bureau. It is 7:08 AM; she will not hit the office until 8:00. She does not even bother to turn on the bathroom light because the room is light enough to wash her face and brush her hair.

Time to throw on some clothes and get some Cheerios. A girl has to look good even if she is late. Maybe heels will substitute for no makeup.

On the way to the refrigerator, she stops to add a new alarm clock to the list of things she was supposed to get on the way home from work.

Let's see…. I can probably get that at the pharmacy when I get Dad's insulin refill. Pharmacy first, then the grocery store to get bread, aluminum foil, and a rotisserie chicken.

With her new executive position, she has not had the time to plan for meals and the pantry is a little bare. Steve usually helps with the shopping but he has been on travel for the last week. Sherry cannot wait until he gets back this afternoon.

Sherry does not realize the electricity is out until she opens the refrigerator to get milk. It is still cool in there but the light does not come on. She has barely enough milk to moisten her Cheerios. Another thing to add to her shopping list. After brushing her teeth (and yes, she does put on lipstick), Sherry gingerly walks down the dark stairs.

I thought we had a flashlight somewhere? Dad should be okay, he usually sleeps until 8:00 anyway and he does not eat much for breakfast or lunch. Surely the power will be back on soon. Man, the garage is dark, too!

Only a little light comes in the window from the people door at the other end of the basement. Sherry pushes the button to open the garage door and nothing happens.

How am I going to get the car out of the garage?

She reaches down and pulls up on the handle. The garage door is solidly locked into place. It will not even budge.

Maybe if I use the remote? Cool, the light in the car came on.

But the remote does not open the garage door either.

Fifteen minutes later, Dad shows up in his

pajamas to open the garage door. "Grab this cord, Sherry. Pull straight down and it disconnects the drive mechanism from the door frame. Then you can open the door the way we used to back in the day." Dad opens the door for Sherry and closes it again after she backs out. The door remains closed but not locked.

Sherry uses her iPhone 5 to speed dial her secretary but there is no answer at the office. She imagines that there will be a meeting room full of irate people waiting for her. Her office is about eleven miles from her house and it normally takes her about twenty minutes. The gas station she frequents is about six miles from her house. With no traffic lights working, it takes her about twenty minutes to just get to the gas station. Fortunately there is no line at the gas station. Unfortunately it is because the gas station is not open. They have no electricity to run their pumps. Sherry's gas gauge is reading less than empty and the amber warning light has been on since she drove home last Friday afternoon.

I think it is time to throw in the towel. I want to be home when Steve gets there. I will just call in sick if I can get someone to answer the phone.

Sherry gets one mile closer to home when her car sputters to a stop in the middle of the road. She did not even have enough warning to coast to the shoulder.

What the heck? Now I am going to have to walk home. Maybe I should not have put on these heels this morning!

Sherry gets out of her car, leaving it in the middle of the road, and locks it. All that she has with her is a purse and a light sweater. She leaves her briefcase on the seat of the passenger side. Continuing in the direction she was heading, Sherry walks on the shoulder of the interstate toward the safety of home. Sherry remembers that there are three more exits before she gets to hers but decides to stay on the interstate. As a jet, obviously destined for the airport, passes overhead, Sherry wonders if Steve is on that particular plane.

By the time Sherry gets to the first exit, her right foot is giving her a fit. She looks down at her feet. The shade of her heels perfectly matches the color of her dress, but they are already scuffed by the little stones and occasional piece of glass that keep her company on the shoulder. The automobile traffic is lighter than she would have expected but it seems that the truckers have not slowed down. Sherry has already almost jumped out of her skin a dozen times when a few truckers blasted their diesel horns at her.

They sure are close. The wind almost knocks me over! Can't they see me on the side of the road?

Sherry considers taking the next exit, but she does not really know how to get home except by the interstate. This part of town is not her stomping ground and she never takes these last couple of exits. Her right heel is burning. The slight slipping of her foot in and out of the shoe has created a water blister just at the back edge of her now ruined heels. She toughs it out and walks on.

I am a chemist and a businesswoman, not Bear Grylls! I was not meant to walk home. And this is not the deep woods. But my foot is killing me! I do not know if I can make the next four or five miles.

Sherry finds a freshly mowed patch of ground between the shoulder of the interstate and the fence that is supposed to keep deer from running out of the woods onto the road. She sits down on the slightly damp grass, pulls off her shoes, and realizes that she is sweating a little bit. She also realizes that she is cold and thirsty. There is a small creek running just on the other side of the fence. Leaving both of her shoes where she was sitting, Sherry gets up and walks over to the fence. As she approaches, a deer leaps up and runs off into the little strip of woods separating the interstate from the old shopping center that she can just barely see.

If that water is clean enough for the deer, it should be clean enough for me. Why am I so thirsty?

As Sherry starts climbing over the fence, two rough looking guys on Harleys slow down to get a better look. Sherry ignores them and they ride on. She hopes they keep on moving. She is starting to get colder as the sweat is evaporating. She has to get on both knees to reach the clean part of the water but it does taste good.

Sherry makes quite a sight as she minces her way on the shoulder toward home. Her arms are crossed over her chest. She is shivering, barefoot, and carrying her shoes in one hand. A small purse is in the other hand. Both of her feet are dirty and the right heel is bleeding. Her knees are filthy and her more-decorative-than-functional sweater is torn on both sleeves. The trucks have not slowed down but Sherry cannot really walk on the rough patches next to the shoulder in her bare feet. At least she can see where to place her feet when walking on the asphalt shoulder. Some truckers still toot their horns as they pass.

Out of sight of any exits or buildings next to the interstate, Sherry hears a motorcycle or two coming up from behind her. She stops and turns around. It looks like those two Harley guys are back and they are slowing down. One has long hair and both have beards.

They have on worn leather clothing and heavy boots. The one with the long hair pulls in front of her and the other one pulls up behind her. They shut down their bikes.

Both of the bikers speak at the same time. The older guy asks, "Are you alone? It looks like you could use some help." The long hair asks, "Where is your car?" Sherry is really frightened and is unable to speak. She grows more fearful when the older biker removes his helmet and she looks at his doo rag. It is black and covered in skull and cross bones. She is reminded of an old pirate movie. The pirate removes his dark glasses and asks her if she needs a ride. Through tears, Sherry pleads, "Please don't hurt me!"

I am an executive. I am smarter than these Neanderthals. I will ride with them and when they slow down, I will jump off and run. I don't have much of an alternative.

Sherry tearfully capitulates and hikes up her skirt to straddle the bike behind the pirate. The pirate gently explains that she will have to wrap her arms around him and lean when he does. For the first mile, she gingerly grasps his sides. After the pirate has to swerve to avoid some debris in the road, she hugs him closely and presses right up against the gang patch on the back of his jacket. It is a coiled snake and says, "Don't tread on me." Fifteen minutes later, two bikes rumble into Sherry's driveway. The bottom of Sherry's skirt is way up around her hips. She dropped one of her shoes somewhere on the interstate but is not going back to get it.

Both the long hair and the pirate shut down their bikes. Sherry hops off the bike and pulls her skirt down to a modest level. The long hair cannot wipe the grin off of his face. Both bikers stay to watch Sherry bend over and open up the garage door. She turns around and tearfully thanks them. They smile, salute their helmets, and crank up their bikes. At the end of the driveway, they turn around and wave at Sherry. She is standing in the garage door opening watching them leave. Dad, fully dressed, joins Sherry in the garage.

Pepper (the prepper) woke up when her alarm sounded at 5:45.

The first thing Pepper notices is the emergency flashlight beaming light against the far wall. It is supposed to come on automatically if there is a power outage. As soon as she hits the snooze button to give herself another nine minutes of sleep, she hears the faint beeping of her computer UPS that is on the other side of the house. Pepper reaches out to turn off the alarm clock; there will be no snoozing for her this morning.

After pulling the flashlight from its holder plugged into the electrical outlet, Pepper turns it off and just looks around. It is dark. Now there is no source of light. She cannot even see any of the red LEDs from her alarm clock. Once again, she silently thanks Paul for insisting she buy the clock with the backup 9-volt battery that kept the alarm working. The power strip LED where she has her Droid plugged in for charging is not lit. Her electric tooth brush charger base is not lit. The only sound she hears in the house is her own breathing and the persistent, yet faint, beep from the UPS.

Pepper walks over and locks her already closed bedroom door. Looking out of her two bedroom windows, all she sees is darkness. Even the street light half way down the block is not lit. No light is coming from any neighbor's windows that she can see. It looks like the power outage is affecting more than just her bedroom or her house. Sherry checks her smart phone. She can get a dial tone and has a Wi-Fi signal, but cannot get on the internet.

Feeling safe in her own home, but still feeling a little uneasy, Pepper decides to check out the rest of the house and see how Mom is doing before she gets dressed for work. Pepper knows the house well enough to be able to navigate without the use of the flashlight. After unlocking the bedroom door and looking down the hallway, she sees a faint glow coming from the stairs leading to where Mom is sleeping.

Of course there would be light, Paul put one of those emergency flashlights in the hallway outside of Mom's bedroom.

There are no LEDs lit in the stereo cabinet or in the kitchen. Both the back door and the front door are still locked. No light is visible through any windows. Pepper decides to check on the computer before she checks on Mom. She slips the flashlight into the pocket of her bathrobe and heads up the stairs. Not surprisingly, the third step gives off a loud creak when she puts her weight on it.

The upstairs bedroom used as their office is not dark. There is an amber glow from the front of the UPS. But the computer cooling fans are not running and the blue LED usually lit on the front of the computer is not on. The lights on the front of the router are lit but the light indicating a good internet connection is amber instead of green. Pepper reaches down and pushes the button to silence the UPS alarm. She is surprised that it did not wake Mom.

Pepper slowly opens the door to Mom's

bedroom. The light from the emergency flashlight in the hallway streams into the room to reveal Mom sitting on the edge of the bed praying. "Good morning, Pepper. At least I think it is morning. That computer thing beeping woke me up and I just did not feel like things were right." Pepper replies. "It is almost six, Mom. It looks like we have a power outage in the neighborhood. The sun should be up soon and I am still planning on going to work if you are going to be okay." Mom laughs. "Pepper, a country girl can survive. I will be fine." For the first time today, Pepper laughs. "I love you, Mom."

Downstairs again, Pepper decides to take a sponge bath instead of a shower. The water pressure is still good and it is still warm enough. She tinkles but does not flush. After getting dressed in a light brown business suit with modest heels, Pepper fixes herself a bowl of Frosted Mini-Wheats. She notes that the refrigerator light does not come on and that if the power does come back on soon, they will lose almost a gallon of milk.

I need to figure out what is going on before I get on the road.

Pepper locates the battery operated radio she bought from Amazon about six months ago. It is still in the original, unopened box. She quickly gets into her stash of batteries and inserts two new AA batteries in the back of the new radio. Nothing happens when she turns it on.

Leaving the dead radio on the kitchen counter, Pepper retrieves her Eton wind up radio and starts cranking. After about five minutes of cranking, she turns it on and is rewarded with Waylon Jennings and Willie Nelson singing something about Mamas and cowboys. Tuning to a talk radio station, she starts listening to the news. It seems there is a regional power outage but the government says there is nothing to worry about and the power should be back on shortly. Neither the talk show host nor Pepper put a lot of faith in what the government says.

Pepper has a few employees at her printing shop and decides that she needs to open up or at least let them know what to do about work. With no power, she will not be able to service customers and she does have some deadlines she is supposed to meet. After a consultation with Mom to make sure she is going to be okay, Pepper rethinks her plans. Mom wants to make sure the neighbors are all okay. It might be too early to check on them now but Mom volunteers to make a few calls after the rest of the world wakes up.

Pepper starts a mental checklist and realizes that it might be better to have some sort of hardcopy checklist in case she ever has to make this sort of travel in the future. Her G19 Glock with a 15 round magazine is stashed safely in its usual holster in the middle of her carry purse. An extra 17 round magazine is in a separate zipper pocket of her purse. She complains to herself about the weight of her purse.

It sure would be nice if I could wear the Glock and the magazines on a belt around my waist. My purse is as heavy now as it was when I was the packhorse for my kids!

Things get more real when she opens the door to the basement stairs and it is pitch black. Fortunately the flashlight is just where it is supposed to be – and it works. It only takes a few minutes to verify that her Get Home Bag (GHB) is in the trunk of her car. Just in case, she puts a case of water bottles in the trunk beside her back pack. Once in the driver's seat, she checks that the road map is in the glove compartment along with a small first aid kit and another flashlight. And of course, the remote does not open the garage door. Paul had her practice the manual operation of the door but that was always with no car in the garage. Now she cannot reach the cord she needs to pull. Pepper finally reaches it using a step ladder and opens the garage door. After backing the car out, she shuts the garage door but cannot figure out how to lock it.

Oh well, Mom has been using that old Remington 870 since before I was born. She can handle herself.

Sherry turns the radio on to the talk show radio station and starts her thirty-minute trip to the print shop.

Besides the traffic lights that are out, there is only one strange happening during the trip. Pepper sees what looks like a woman she has seen before in church with her skirt around her waist hugging some Hell's Angel guy like she is a biker babe on the back of a Harley. They are making good time in the opposite direction.

The Pepper's Print Shop sign is dark and the only two cars in the parking lot are her employees waiting for her to get there. They see her coming and jump out of their cars. After some excited greetings, all three of them enter the shop together. The computer used for billing has been automatically shut down by the attached UPS and nothing else is lit. There is sufficient light coming in the front window to light up the front part of the store and everything looks in order. While the two employees try to call the customers with impending deadlines, Pepper makes a sign for the front door. None of the customers can be reached because the only customer contact information is on the shutdown computer. The handmade sign lets the other two employees and any customers who come in know that Pepper's Print Shop will be closed until the power comes back on.

Pepper gives each of her employees a six-pack of water bottles and sends them home with instructions to come back when the power comes on. Locking up the store, she gets in her own car and heads for home. She figures that in an hour, she will be sitting at the kitchen table having a little cold lunch with Mom.

Pepper's normal trip home is not normal at all. She is forced off the interstate three exits early because of an accident or something that is now blocking all lanes. She feels fortunate that she noticed it before it was too late to take the exit. Many other cars are stuck on the interstate and are unable to back up to the exit ramp. Ever since they put those cable barriers up in the median area, there is no way to turn around even if it was legal.

Once off the interstate, Pepper recognizes where she is. The power is out here, too. Pepper does not want to go through the bad area of town since the traffic lights are not working. She pulls off to the side of the road at a construction site to activate an alternative route in her car's built-in GPS. A galvanized roofing nail smoothly enters the sidewall of her right front tire as she gets back on the road. It takes another two blocks before the tire pressure monitoring system light on her dashboard turns amber and the alarm sounds. Pepper does not worry because both her father and Paul made sure she knew how to change a flat tire.

That took longer than expected. There goes my lunch with Mom! Maybe we will have to have a cold supper.

With the damaged tire in the trunk along with her GHB and two six-packs of bottled water, Pepper starts off again toward home. Stuff happens. She makes it another two miles. The valve stem on the spare fails by ejecting a crucial part and the air rapidly escapes causing Pepper to pull off onto the shoulder of an empty country road. There are no reception bars on her phone, and Pepper has not seen a car on this road since she turned on it. All that she can see around her are cotton fields with no buildings.

Pepper makes sure the car doors are locked and turns off the engine. She pulls the map from the glove compartment but cannot find out where she is. She knows generally where she is but needs to know more specifically if she is going to walk home. There are no route or street signs visible. After studying the map for a while, she decides to start the car again and use the GPS. The GPS tells her exactly where she is and she plans her four mile walk home.

Checking her surroundings again, Pepper gets out of the car to retrieve her GHB. This time she gets in the back seat. Off comes the suit and Pepper quickly dresses in a pair of jeans and a shirt. This time her leather belt holds the G19 holster on her right hip and the magazine pouch on her left hip. A light jacket covers them from public view. A pair of FITs socks goes on her feet before she puts on her light purple hiking boots. Right before she gets out of the car for the last time, she writes a note to anyone who might find the car and leaves it on the dashboard. Her briefcase goes in the trunk where the GHB used to be. Her purse and two water bottles go into her pack. A CREE LED flashlight goes in the front pocket of her jacket. Pepper puts on the pack and then has to take it off again when she remembers she forgot to put on a hat. After adjusting the pack on her back one more time, she rechecks that the car is locked. With the map in her hand, she heads off toward home.

Two hours later, Pepper tries to open her own garage door. It will not move. Going around to the front door, she pushes the doorbell with no success. Mom has heard the activity, saw Pepper through the window and opens the door. Mom, with a shotgun in her left hand, welcomes home Pepper with a big hug. "Sorry, honey. I locked the garage door after you left."

HOW TO START

How to start is a very interesting question. Some folks take a more structured approach and seem to think that you must know what you are preparing for before you can make any preparations at all. I do not subscribe to that philosophy. Later on, that makes a lot of sense. In the beginning, start by starting. That is not very helpful, or is it? Hmmmm. Keep it simple in the beginning. It will save you money, time, frustration, and still get you toward where you want to go. You do not need to know what the ultimate survival rifle is to start taking some responsibility for your own welfare. So here is the simple start. Beans, bullets, and Band-Aids. For those of us who may need more of an explanation, this is not to be taken literally. Everyone can remember the letter "B" and it can be helpful to think about your preparations in those three buckets (see, another "B") or categories.

Beans

This is the food and water category. Many folks are only nine meals, or three days, from starvation. We all need food and water to live. It does not have to be an end of civilization event to cause an interruption in our food and water supply. Think about a hurricane, a flood, or even the loss of a job. You do not need to purchase a two-year's supply of wheat to feel like you are moving in the right direction. Quite simply, store what you eat and eat what you store. Back to the question at hand, "How to start?" Storing food and water is a multi-level process. My recommendation is that you start in the grocery store. One of our family rules might help you and will have very little felt impact on your budget. We buy one extra thing (like a can) every time we go into the grocery store for any reason. Many times this ends up being a "buy one, get one free" item. Soon these extra cans start adding up without you even noticing. Another rule we follow involves a Sharpie and has given us some perspective on our shopping requirements. Every can we buy gets labeled with the month and year of purchase on the bottom of the can. Every box we buy gets labeled on the upper right-hand corner. This helps us rotate the food and lets us know how long it takes from purchase to consumption. And folks, buy some water bottles. Remember, this is just a place to start.

Bullets

This is the protection category. You may be an anti-gun person. That does not matter because there are other folks (for instance, bad guys) who are not anti-gun. You still need to protect yourself and your family. Once again, how do you get started? Here I think you start out with education. There are plenty of courses around that you might want to take. Your local adult community education system might have something you are interested in. The NRA teaches a non-firearm, personal protection course called, "Refuse to Be a Victim." The NRA also teaches basic courses about pistol, rifle, and shotgun. Or get a book and read. But start somewhere. When seconds count, policemen are only minutes away. Be responsible for yourself. And folks, lock your doors and keep your eyes open.

Band-Aids

This is the medical/doctor/dentist category. You do not have to be Dr. Ben Carson to be a prepper. Here I recommend you start with a first aid kit for your house and one for each car. Then think about some education.

When was the last time you had a first aid or CPR course? Many of us use prescription drugs. You might think about how you are managing those prescriptions so that a brief interruption in the supply chain does not endanger your health. Will you doctor or health care plan allow for a 90-day rather than a 30-day prescription? And folks, get some exercise.

Beans, Bullets, and Band-Aids all cost money. And they all have some sort of risk (i.e. shelf-life, fire, theft). There is one thing that does not have the same type of associated risk. Your brain. You might think about what you know how to do and what you might have to know how to do. The acquisition of skills might just be something you want to start. And that folks, is another story.

WATER

Water is one of the critical survival preparation items you need to think about in advance. It is both one of the easiest and one of the hardest items to deal with. If you go without drinking for three days, you are going to die. You need water to drink, to prepare food, to wash yourself, to wash dishes, and to wash clothes. You also need water for your plants, pets, and livestock. Water weighs about eight (8) pounds per gallon. One well-known thumb rule is to drink eight 8-ounce glasses (64 ounces) of water a day. Another well-known thumb rule is to divide your weight in half and drink that many ounces. A 128 pound person would need to drink 64 ounces of water per day. I weigh considerably more than 128 pounds. Thank God that sweet tea counts as water.

Of course the amount of water you need to drink is highly dependent on your size, your activity level, your health, and the environmental conditions. If you get to a state where your mouth feels dry and you really need water, you are already in a dehydrated state. It is better to drink all along and not get into that state in the first place. Do not forget to check your pee color. It should be light yellow and clear. If it is dark yellow or orange, you are dehydrated and need water. If it is brown, go to the hospital.

We can combine some water demands such as when we wash dishes or do laundry. While we may be able to combine some needs and efforts, we cannot combine drinking water. We still need to estimate what our total water needs are per day per person. The prevalent thumb rule is that we need one gallon of water per person per day for all water demands.

Here are some quick conversions for you.

- 1 quart = 32 ounces = 2 pounds
- 2 quarts = 64 ounces = 4 pounds
- 4 quarts = 1 gallon = 132 ounces = 8 pounds

Those conversions into weight are provided for a reason. Imagine if you are bugging out with a family of four for three days. Four gallons of water per day times three days equals 12 gallons of water you need to carry on your back. This makes your BOB weigh 96 pounds even before you put anything else in it.

God provides water for us. And water does not have an expiration date. That is the easy part. The hard part is that all of that water may not be fresh or clean water. It may not be in the right place at the right time. And it is heavy. That is the hard part.

Water Resource Survey

Before you get too excited about collecting water, you need to evaluate where the water already is. Take some time to conduct a survey and make some notes. See what "native" sources of water are already there without out you having to take any extra action. Include pictures and maps if you think that will prove useful in the future.

Water Inside Your House

Every house will be different, but you probably already have plenty of water in your house. Use your survey effort to help you identify the source, estimate the volume or capacity, determine the classification (i.e. potable, washing, cooking, and firefighting) and make an initial stab at how you are going to gain use of the water. You might find the [A004] Water Resource Survey (Inside) template useful. A few examples are included to give you the idea.

My aunt used to live in a house with no running water and an outhouse. I loved to visit but it was cold in the winter. The hand pump was on the unheated, screened-in back porch. Even they had some sources of water within the house. They always had ice cubes of some type. In an emergency, they could melt the ice cubes and drink that water right away. They usually had a pitcher of water for drinking in the refrigerator. Both of these sources would not last very long and neither were a good source for firefighting. Unless their well went dry, they were better off than many folks on city water with no well and no water pressure in their lines.

Here is a partial list of potential "native" water sources in homes.

- Ice cubes
- Frozen jugs of water in freezer
- Toilet bowls
- Toilet tanks (back of toilet)
- House piping – can drain to low point
- Hot water heater
- Aquarium

Some of these native sources can be consumed without any other steps needed. Others can be used as a firefighting agent with no other steps needed. You might want to purify your aquarium water before drinking it.

Water Outside Your Home

Water outside your home can be grouped into multiple areas. Water sources may exist in your own yard, a neighbor's yard, your neighborhood, or in your OP AREA. It could be valuable to take a purposeful walking and driving trip to survey the water sources in your OP AREA. Permission is always nice. If you are friendly with your neighbor, they may agree in advance to allow you to draw water from their swimming pool or pond. All other things being equal, it is better to draw from a running rather than a stagnant natural water source.

Here is a partial list of potential "native" water sources outside homes.

- Downspout collection barrels
- Swimming pool
- Pond, lake, or reservoir
- Creek
- Fire hydrant
- Municipal water tower

Water Barrels

You might think hard about putting multiple 55-gallon water barrels in your third-story apartment. If you stack one above the other, you will have an 880-pound weight hovering just above the breakfast table of the nice folks on the second floor. But water barrels in general are not a bad idea. They are extremely hard to move around and can be hard to get the water out of. Gravity drains the water only down to the spigot. If the spigot is just at the bottom edge, you cannot get a catch container under it. One alternative is to put the barrel on its side and use the spigot like you see the beer kegs tapped in the movies. Another alternative is to purchase a manual or siphon pump. You can also put the barrel on a raised platform.

You still have to fill these barrels. It might be nice to have them filled automatically. That is totally possible. Rain collection barrels are designed to do just that. You have to consider the roofing materials where the rain hits and then runs into the downspouts. A metal or clay tile roof would be best. Amazon, ebay, Sams, and Costco all sell rain barrels. A simple downspout modification allows you to collect all of the rainwater you want. The overflow can be directed into your yard, into your garden, or daisy-chained into more barrels. RLP recommends you get a darker colored rain barrel as light passing through the barrel can cause considerable algae growth in the water. An urn shaped, terra cotta colored plastic rain barrel may keep your neighbors happier. A nice rain barrel can cost about $100.

Water Bob

This is not the Bob who did not have any cash at the Salt Lick. Think water bed. A Water Bob is a plastic bladder that holds about 100 gallons of water. It costs around $20. The bladder lies in your bathtub and is filled by the bathtub spigot. It usually comes with a manual pump to extract the water. Your bathtub is designed to hold that kind of weight (800 pounds) and if it leaks, you are safe. Naturally you probably cannot always leave your Water Bob in place. This is a preparation action you take when you have advance notice of an upcoming emergency such as a hurricane.

Regular Water Bottles

If you have more money than sense, you can have literally a ton of regular water bottles. Just remember, Evian spelled backwards is naive. Regular water bottles do have their place. They just do not make sense for large volumes of water. Some studies suggest that there are issues with both long-term storage of water in regular water bottles and the reuse of regular water bottles. Concerns center on the leaching of cancer-causing materials from the plastic into the water and the bacteria and fungi that can linger in non-sanitized bottles. Of course, the International Bottled Water Association refutes all of these claims.

Reusable Water Bottles

Lexan, Nalgene, and other polycarbonate sport bottles are ubiquitous. They make sense if you clean them properly and do not consider them a long-term water storage option. Many folks want to make sure they are BPA free.

Milk Jug Water Storage

No, do not do it. Environmental concerns led the milk container industry to manufacture biodegradable gallon milk jugs. This means that the water you store in the cleaned out, decomposing, milk jug is going to leak out when you least expect it. Water in the wrong place at the wrong time can do some serious damage.

Yes, do it. RLP recommends you keep your freezer full. It is more efficient and uses less electricity. It also helps maintain the freshness of your food if you have a power failure. So what do you do if you do not have enough food to keep your freezer full? The answer is to fill some properly cleaned out, one-gallon milk jugs with water and freeze them. You will have some water, and ice, in reserve and keep your food colder longer when you have a power failure.

Soda and Juice Bottle Water Storage

Budget-minded or earth-centric folks may want to recycle and reuse the two and three liter bottles that juice and sodas come in. They are designed for long term storage and are easy to handle. When properly cleaned, they can save you money and maybe save your life.

Water Treatment

If you trust the municipality you get your water from, there is no need to treat the water coming out of your tap. But what happens when you have a flood or hurricane and the sewage treatment plant overflows into the potable water distribution plant? And what about that water from your downspout water barrels? I hate to break this to you, but birds use your roof as a toilet. You need to know how to treat water to make it safe.

You can certainly boil water, but boiling alone does not make it safe, nor does it make it taste good.

Boiling can kill the biological contaminants. It cannot remove radioactivity, petroleum products, or dirt. And remember those bacteria and protozoa (like Giardia) that you killed by boiling? They are still there; they are just dead and you are drinking their little tiny bodies. Actually, boiling can release some toxins from blue-green algae that are much more toxic than cyanide. Chances are you are probably safe boiling your tap water if you need to. While the internet experts say anywhere from 3 to 30 minutes, the EPA says a real boil for one minute is sufficient. A staged process, which may include filtering out the big chunks, boiling, and treating with a charcoal filter may be your best bet.

One day RLP returned home to find several unopened regular water bottles in the trash. Why did MrsRLP put them in the trash? They had exceeded their expiration date! Wake up folks, water has been around a long time; it does not expire! Many times expiration dates are just marketing tools. There may be some wisdom in watching the length of time water is stored in plastic containers that leach out chemicals. The International Bottled Water Association will probably tell you that the hazardous chemicals are still at a safe level until the expiration date. I do not know about you, but the RLP family would rather not experience the hazardous chemicals at all.

However, we sometimes purposely introduce hazardous chemicals to take care of other problems. Biological contamination can really mess up your day. Mankind has a love/hate relationship with chlorine. In general, chlorine is not good for you. A heavy dose will kill you outright. Smaller doses can mess up your hair, skin, increase the risk of certain ailments, and even increase your chances of developing allergies. Even smaller doses can keep you alive by killing viruses and bacteria that would otherwise have killed you. Most hazardous chlorine exposure comes through your skin (like when you are swimming in a public pool or taking a shower in your house), not through drinking treated water.

When you store water for a long time, you stand a risk of having unwanted bacteria growth in the water. Treatment of the water when you store it can prevent or mitigate that risk. Treatment with chlorine is probably the best answer. But you cannot just waltz into the local Publix and buy a bottle of chlorine. Or can you?

Household bleach has not been approved by our trustworthy government for human consumption. However, in an emergency situation, you can use unscented, plain, bleach to treat your water. Fundamentally, household bleach is just sodium hypochlorite. We would hope the manufacturer has no impurities in the bleach. One gallon of bleach can treat 3,800 gallons of clear water. Use eight (8) drops of bleach for every one gallon of clear water. Make sure you sanitize the storage container before you put the water in it. The water like this that you drink should have a slight bleach odor. If you check your stored water down the road and there is no bleach odor at all, you can treat it again. If you absolutely know what you are doing, you can also use solid pool chemicals (sodium hypochlorite) rather than liquid household bleach. If you search the internet, you will find other chemical treatment recommendations including Aquamira, Potable Aqua, and various chlorine dioxide tablets.

Water on the Move

There are a variety of ways you can treat water while on the move. Many folks carry a BPA-free, Sport Berkey Portable Water Purifier sold all over the internet. You can feel safe filling this up from a creek in the woods or from the water supply in a third-world country and drinking straight from the bottle. Interestingly, the $20 Berkey Sport Bottle also removes the chlorine.

An even more portable solution is the LifeStraw Personal Water Filter. This straw allows you to safely drink directly from the water source but does not store the water so you can walk around. The LifeStraw runs from $15 to $20.

Water Filters

British Berkefeld gravity water filters have been the king of water filters since the early 1800s. Affectionately known as a Berkey, this water purifier uses cleanable and replaceable ceramic elements. They require no electricity and have no moving parts. Unless the disaster includes a failure of gravity, the Berkey will work for you. Most Berkeys have room for up to four elements. More elements mean higher flow rate, not cleaner water. The older design elements are white Super Sterasyl filters that still are fabulous. The newer black elements (with some manufacturing problems when they first came out) will also remove heavy metals and MTBEs. RLP highly recommends that you buy a Berkey for your family as perhaps your first prepper purchase. The newer black elements are preferred. Berkeys are not cheap ($200-$300).

Poor Man's Berkey

The Internet Prepper [L099] http://www.internetprepper.com/ sells a Ceramic Water Filter Kit for $30, at a fraction of the cost of a Berkey. It is designed to work with two food grade, plastic, 5-gallon buckets that you supply and then drill your own holes. They do not advertise a capacity in terms of total number of gallons filtered but do say it should last between one and two years. RLP has both the Berkey and this filter kit. But then again, you probably already knew that.

Survival Still

God purifies water better than we can. But we can learn from how he does it. He evaporates the ocean, leaving all of the salt and contaminants behind, and rains down clean water on both the just and the unjust. [L098] http://survivalstill.com/ sells a very innovative still that works on your stove top or grill. Even if you do not buy the still, the website has access to a 27-page booklet on FEMA and Red Cross guidelines for purifying water in a disaster situation. The survival still is highly recommended by RLP.

Bad Tasting Water

We can imagine a situation where you might sanitize your water but where it is still discolored or even tastes bad. What do you do now? Hold your nose and drink it? We want to thrive, not just survive. One possible solution is to carry some drink mix with you. I can personally testify to the good taste of a product called Zipfizz. It comes in a plastic, sealed, individualized tube suitable for mixing with 16-22 ounces of water. It does fizz a little so do not pour the powdered contents into a 20 ounce water bottle without drinking some water first. You will have a volcano on your hands. The zip comes from the vitamins. For instance, it has 41,667% of your daily B12. Yes, that is right, 42 thousand percent.

If you need an energy drink as well as to mask the color or flavor, this is a good choice. The variety pack has pink lemonade, orange soda, and grape. The grape reminds me of Grapico. Costco sells it in boxes of 20 or 30 tubes at around $1 each tube. It is sold on Amazon (more expensive) and from the Zipfizz website. The website has additional flavors.

There is an advertised "best if used by" date, but it is pretty well sealed and protected. I think the benefits will far out last the "expiration" date. Buy a box. Put a tube or two in each BOB and a couple in your glove compartment.

MiO Water Enhancer (liquid) is another choice with no energy drink benefits (no calories, no caffeine). One 1.6 ounce bottle flavors about 24 glasses.

FOOD

Food is one category of your preparations that can make your family mad at you if you have not done things properly. For instance, RLP hates beets. If all we had stored was beets, I would not be happy. In addition, beets do not provide an adequately balanced diet. A balanced diet is a key element to survival. There are many documented cases of "rabbit starvation." A balanced diet is sometimes not available to wild animals either. This happens particularly during the winter. In some parts of Alabama we have too many deer. They eat all of the normal deer food then consume all of the foods that other animals normally eat. Rabbits cannot get a balanced diet. They provide protein but are too lean. Man does live by protein alone. Without fat, he will die. Explorers have been known to try and rely on rabbits alone but ended up dying by starvation. Research revealed they had plenty of rabbits, just not enough fat.

Other folks believe they will be able to survive just by going out in the woods and harvesting what they need to eat. This logic is faulty on many levels. First, it is illegal. For instance, deer season in Alabama is from the Saturday before Thanksgiving to January 31. Granted, we are allowed two deer per day. Take it from an experienced hunter; you will not be able to harvest two deer per day. You will probably not even see two deer every day. And how would you process and store 80-some deer for the rest of the year. What about all of the bubbas out there thinking they will do the same thing? You are probably as likely to get shot as to shoot your own deer. And even with 1.5 million deer in Alabama alone, how long will they last with everyone shooting everything in sight?

Sustainable grocery stores are not happening

either. According to the United States Department of Agriculture, tomatoes travel an average distance of 1,369 miles from the field to your plate. Lettuce travels an average distance of 2,055 miles. Even the slightest interruption of travel routes or fuel supplies could empty grocery stores when they are needed the most. In Alabama, even a mention of snow or ice causes all grocery stores to empty themselves of milk and bread within hours.

Some writers opine that we live only three days until a revolution. Their reasoning is that the average family has only nine meals available in their home. Lack of food causes revolutions. Taxes may not cause a revolution, but no food on your children's plates can get your attention.

So what is the answer? The answer is to store some food. Some folks consider this hoarding. RLP considers it real life prepping. The folks who have stored food are more likely to be able to share with those folks who have not. In time of scarcity, they will also not be competing with other folks who have not planned ahead. The answer raises many new questions. How do you acquire the food? What food do you acquire? How do you store the food?

Enemies of food are temperature, oxygen, and moisture. Fats turn rancid with oxygen and surprisingly, oxygen can cause foods to oxidize. Bugs cannot live without oxygen or moisture for very long. There are a variety of ways to get rid of oxygen. One of the ways is to use an oxygen absorber. An oxygen absorber is essentially a permeable envelope containing iron that can oxidize. For iron, that means rust. The oxygen is trapped in the rust and is removed from the closed environment. For those wondering minds, that is how a hand warmer works. The oxidation (rusting) of the iron is an exothermal reaction meaning it generates heat. This also means you could use a hand warmer in a pinch.

Another way you can get rid of oxygen is by getting rid of the regular air which is made of 21% oxygen. You can suck it all out using a vacuum system or you can replace the free oxygen with carbon dioxide. Frozen carbon dioxide is called dry ice. When melted, it does not add water moisture, it adds carbon dioxide. Carbon dioxide is heavier than air and displaces the regular air (containing the free oxygen) over the lip of the container into the environment.

One can get rid of the moisture by dehydrating or freeze drying the food. Bugs can be killed by freezing them. Freezing food is not the same as freeze drying the food. Freeze drying food is not within the capability of most real life preppers.

All dry pack foods, particularly those purchased in boxes (like macaroni and cheese) already contain live bugs (like weevils) and their eggs. Normally you eat them without noticing. In fact, they may even be good for you. From personal experience, we learned that these types of foods (stored on the shelf for long enough) will produce at least one crop of weevils if left untreated. The weevils will make their way out of the box and gravity will insure they migrate to other boxes stored on lower shelves. One solution here is to store the boxes in plastic shoeboxes. Gravity and slippery plastic keep the weevils in the shoeboxes and makes cleanup a lot easier. The shoeboxes also facilitate better organization. A better solution is to treat the box immediately after purchase. Freeze the box for two to four days immediately after purchase. This will kill the live bugs but may not kill the eggs. Wait two to four days or so at room temperature and then freeze the box for another two to four days to kill the newly hatched bugs. It may not be perfect, but it works better than nothing. Besides, you did not know any better before. You have always eaten them.

Commercially Canned Goods

Most folks look at canned goods as the first step in storing food. After all, they already store food in cans. RLP made a commitment in our early days that we did not leave the grocery store without one extra can designated for storage. This virtually was not even visible to our budget. And since we usually took advantage of two-for-one sales, we followed the critical principle of storing what we eat. We bought no two-for-one cans of beets.

There are some downsides to having canned goods for food storage. Some cans are lined with a plastic called Bisphenol A or BPA. BPA has been linked with some diseases in humans and the Federal Drug Administration (FDA) is unsure of the maximum safe levels. The RLP family considers zero the maximum safe level of BPA.

MrsRLP requested a number of shelving units for the extra canned good storage. The flat storage shelves came with their own problems in addition to taking up space. When new canned goods were purchased, they were put on the front of the shelves and the older canned goods were pushed toward the back. When accessing the needed canned goods for consumption, they came from the front of the shelf.

RLP came to the rescue by designing and building a can rotator. It saved floor space and automatically rotated the canned goods. Built in the shape of a chevron, new cans were placed on the outside where they rolled to the inside for pickup. Here is a picture of the partially filled can rotator affixed to the concrete basement wall. Cans are grouped so that the same food is stored on the same shelf. Individual shelves are labeled with a 3x5 card.

What you may notice is writing on the bottom of the cans. Although virtually all cans are already labeled with an expiration date, RLP does not believe them. They are also hard to read. We use several methods to identify length of storage and to ensure safety. First, older cans roll down toward the middle and canned goods for consumption are always taken from the bottom (center/middle). Second, all purchases (including boxed goods) are labeled with the month and year of purchase on the bottom using a Sharpie. This allows us to manage our purchases since we know how long it takes from purchase until consumption. The beets we bought were purchased in September of 1897. The quick visibility into what our canned goods inventory is allows us to take advantage of bulk deals and sales.

The food safety is primarily a matter of senses: common sense, seeing, hearing, and smelling. If the can is visibly rusty, swollen, dented, or bulged, it becomes a candidate for disposal. If the can makes a hiss when opened, there is probably something wrong. If it looks or smells bad, it probably is. Where possible, we avoid purchase of canned goods that have the easy open tabs built into the lids. High and varying temperatures are enemies of all types of food storage including canned goods. The basement is underground and the temperature is relatively a low, constant temperature. There is no moisture exposure to the cans that can cause rust. I have known folks that dip or brush wax on their canned goods to make them last longer. In general, taste and palatability last much longer than nutritional value. But even nutritional value does not disappear overnight.

In 1865, the Steamboat Bertrand sunk in the Missouri River in what is now known as Nebraska. In 1969, over 100 years later, it was salvaged. In the salvage were a number of canned goods that had been under water the entire time. In 1974, the National Food Processors Association (NFPA) analyzed the cans of oysters, brandied peaches, plum tomatoes, honey, and mixed vegetables. Some of the color and taste was degraded. Everything was safe to eat. Significant vitamin C and vitamin A was lost (if they knew what they were when canned) but protein and calcium values were compatible with today's standards. Note that canning processes and standards were different 100 years ago. How sure can we be that currently established "expiration dates" have significant real value? The RLP family takes advantage of approaching expiration dates to donate food to needy families.

Home Canned Foods

Do you trust commercially canned foods? Do you know where the product comes from, what additives have been mixed with your food, or if the best of the food has been reserved for you? If not, you may want to consider home canning. There are three major types of home canning. One is called dry pack canning that the RLP family does not normally deal with. The others are hot water bath canning and pressure canning. Like most real life preppers, we started out with hot water bath canning. There were reasons for this. Primarily, MrsRLP was told by her mother that pressure canning was dangerous because pressure cookers exploded. Little did we know that some foods can only be pressure canned. Low acid foods, such as spaghetti sauce must be pressure canned. High acid foods such as jams and jellies can be water bath canned. The canning recipe will specify which type of canning is required. And yes, meats can be canned.

Water bath canning can be done easily on your regular stove top. In essence, you raise the temperature and pressure in your partially sealed Ball or Mason jar through total immersion in very hot water and the jar lid seals as the jar cools off. RLP highly recommends *The Ball Complete Book of Home Preserving* [L052] http://www.amazon.com/Ball-Complete-Book-Home-Preserving/dp/0778801314/ref=sr_1_1?ie=UTF8&qid=1392242237&sr=8-1&keywords=ball+canning+book available everywhere, including Amazon.

All pressure cookers do not explode. RLP highly recommends the line of All American Pressure Cookers/Canners [L053] http://www.allamericanpressurecookers.com/. Particularly look at the canning models such as the 915 and 921 with multiple closing devices. They are worth every penny. Good raw beef is delicious pressure canned. Canning pressure cookers have only two or three inches of water at the bottom and do not cover the tops of the jars. Normally these canners cannot be used on glass surface stove tops.

Vacuum Packing

So why is vacuum packing included in the food prepping category? Because this is real life prepping! One can help extend the storage life of food by simply vacuum packing the food. Meat (like freshly processed venison) can be vacuum packed before being frozen and it will prevent or at least mitigate freezer burn. There are some things you do not want to vacuum pack. Take it from real life experiences (not all mine, thankfully). When I was growing up, my mother would purchase extra loaves of regular bread and then freeze them for later use. Sometimes they would attract moisture before freezing and that would make them soggy when defrosted. More recently, I had a friend who was trying to freeze some bread for "long term" storage. She decided to vacuum pack the loaves to make them last even longer. Be aware that a good vacuum sealer will suck the air out of the inside of the loaf. The regular loaf of bread became a very flat loaf of bread that resembled Pita bread more than a regular loaf.

Note that many vacuum packers come with an automatic shutoff mechanism. When it draws enough vacuum, it shuts itself off and heat seals the plastic bag. This works perfectly for a deer tenderloin. Other vacuum packers also come with a manual shutoff. When the loaf of bread you are vacuum packing gets flat enough, manually shut if off then manually push the SEAL button to seal the plastic bag. There are a few other features you want to look for in vacuum packers. The width can be a significant criterion. Another useful feature is a tubing fitting so you can vacuum pack Mason jars with the right lid adapters and supplied plastic tubing. RLP recommends vacuum sealers made by FoodSaver, particularly [L050] http://www.foodsaver.com/vacuum-sealers/T000-33270-P.html#start=19&sz=12 although a different model may meet your needs better. FoodSaver and other brand vacuum sealers are also sold by Amazon.

RLP mentioned sealing the plastic bags. RLP recommends that you stick primarily to the branded plastic bags supplied by the vacuum packer. Yes, you can seal up a plastic/Mylar potato chip bag. But first consider the implications of vacuum packing the chips. For larger items, you can purchase and use Mylar bags. Thus the criterion for the width of the sealer. The vendor's branded plastic bags come in two styles. The first is a stack of pre-sized plastic bags. Think pint or quart size bags with three sides already heat sealed. Here you are limited to the length of the contents. The second style is actually not a bag at all but rather a roll with two sides (the outside edges) factory heat sealed. You use the vacuum packer to seal one end of the roll, pull to desired length, cut it, and then you have a customized length bag. After using the vacuum feature to suck out all of the air, it heat seals like a factory manufactured bag. Many times, combo packs of factory bags and rolls are sold in special deals on the manufacturer's website or at Costco and Sam's.

There is another way to seal extra-wide bags (primarily Mylar bags) but the vacuum feature is sorely lacking. It can be done, it is just difficult. You may want to seal up the Mylar bags without all of the vacuum packing. RLP used to recommend the Harbor Freight 15-1/2 inch Electric Impulse Sealer but evidently they do not sell it online anymore. Sears sells a similar 16 inch impulse sealer [L051] http://www.sears.com/impulse-sealer-16-inch-electrical-impulse-bag-sealer/p-SPM158176932.

In real life, you have choices. Let's say that you want to store five gallons of rice in a plastic bucket. You can decide to use a food grade, clean plastic bucket to store the rice. No problem. On the other hand, you may opt for an extra layer of protection by placing a properly sized Mylar bag in the bucket. Use oxygen absorbers or dry ice to displace the air while adding the rice, then seal up the Mylar bag. Consider the implications of getting into the rice for consumption the first time. Air is let into the nicely protected rice and from that point on, the rice is more at risk. Another option is to vacuum pack and seal up smaller, individual bags of rice suitably sized for one meal or just a few meals. Stack all of the sealed bags in the five gallon bucket and you get the best of both worlds. You may even choose to add appropriately sized bags of beans to the same bucket since you might be serving beans along with that rice.

Remember reading about the RLP family purchasing an extra can of food each time we went to the grocery store? Sometimes we cheated. After a while, it became hard to pick out that extra can of food. So we diversified. Sometimes it became a block of canning wax or a plastic bag of soup mix with some type of beans and a seasoning pack. The instructions for the soup mix were printed on the plastic bag. We wanted to keep the instructions but still vacuum pack the soup mix. Vacuum packing a sealed plastic bag inside another plastic bag was an exercise in futility. However, we figured out a solution that worked. Using a sharp knife or scissors, we made some small slices in the original packing material, preserving the written instructions. The vacuum sealer effectively removed all traces of air from both bags and heat sealed the required outside bag.

There are other reasons to have a vacuum sealer that have little or nothing to do with food. The RLP family uses ours for a variety of purposes. Be aware that sharp edges on the contents can compromise the vacuum seal by puncturing the plastic bags. If you decide to store materials for barter, you may also decide to vacuum pack them for longer life. A carton of cigarettes may become more valuable after the schumer hits the fan but cigarettes do not last that long when exposed to the air. A small section of paper towel draped over the sharp corners of the carton can help preserve the integrity of the plastic bag that contains the carton. Be aware that a carton of cigarettes can flatten out the same way as my friend's loaf of bread. Think of other things you can vacuum seal to keep out air, water, or dirt. Items you may consider are: boxes of kitchen matches, ammunition, a pistol, toilet paper for your GHB , BOB, batteries, a flash light and batteries not yet installed, spare parts, etc.

Dehydrated Foods

Normally preppers on the same journey consider dehydrating food shortly after considering vacuum packing. MrsRLP was making beef jerky in the oven long before prepping was cool. But an oven is not the optimum solution for dehydrating food. Dehydrating food can effectively preserve some foods and certainly can make it more portable. A homemade dehydrator can be put together cheaper than a commercial device but it is probably not worth the savings. Extra features such as rotating trays, timers, constant temperatures and adequately circulated air make them well worth their money. RLP recommends the Excalibur line of dehydrators [L054] http://www.excaliburdehydrator.com/. Size it based on how often you think you will use it. Bigger is usually better. Let me give you a real life hint here. Do not try to dehydrate onions for your first experiment.

Freeze Dried Foods

As previously mentioned, home freeze drying food is out of reach of the *Real Life Prepper*. This does not at all mean that you should avoid freeze dried foods. Although more expensive, they are usually tastier, easier to prepare, maintain higher nutritional value, and last longer. Any serious *Real Life Prepper* should highly consider freeze dried foods as a vital component of preparations. In real life, they can be used on hiking and camping trips.

In the commercial process, foods (including entire meals such as casseroles) are flash frozen and then dried in a vacuum process to remove the water without it going through the liquid state. This preserves nutrients and causes it to taste like the real thing when reconstituted in boiling water.

Although there are several good brands, RLP has a lot of experience with and recommends the Mountain House line of freeze dried foods [L055] http://www.mountainhouse.com/. You do not have to purchase Mountain House freeze dried foods directly from Mountain House. They are available everywhere.

Most freeze dried food packages come in of two formats. The first format, and most expensive is smaller foil packs. Foil pouches have an advertised shelf life of 10 years when maintained below 75 degrees. You can add the boiling water directly to the foil pack and eat out of the pack. The other format is a #10 can. Here you measure out the desired portion into a pot and add the boiling water. This is less expensive but requires you to open up an entire can for even one meal. A #10 can of beef stew has 10 servings and has a 25-year advertised shelf life. They also recommend using up the entire #10 can within one week after opening.

LTS (Long Term Storage)

What if you wanted to store food for a very long time? Around 2500 BC, some wheat was stored in the pyramids so the dead pharaoh could eat something if he got hungry. Around 2000 AD, some of the wheat was studied and even planted. It germinated and became viable wheat plants! Wheat is one of the truly long term storage foods and is very versatile. Some folks eat steamed wheat seeds for breakfast. Others sprout the wheat and eat the sprouts. Others grind the wheat to flour and make bread. Wheat seeds do not have to be frozen or dehydrated. Just keep it dry, dark, and cool. Processed flour does not have a very long shelf life and can be harmful to humans.

Ever wonder how to make flour? You do not want to make it the same way that the big suppliers make it to sell in the store. It is highly processed to extend the shelf life. Most of the good stuff in wheat is taken out and sold for animal food. The un-good stuff is sold for human consumption after they bleach it and enrich it with other chemicals. There is an easy way to make flour yourself and a less easy way. The easy way requires electricity. The less easy way requires muscle power. But what are you going to do with no electricity? RLP highly recommends the electrically powered Wonder Mill [L061] http://www.thewondermill.com/ that can process 100 pounds of flour an hour. RLP also highly recommends the muscle powered Country Living Grain Mill [L062] http://countrylivinggrainmills.com/ available in many places including Amazon.

RLP's first experience with a manual grain mill was not a pretty site. The RLP family was visiting a like-minded family who had earlier purchased a different type of manual grain mill but had not yet used it. Of course, we had to try it during our visit. It was hard to operate and really needed to be fixed down tightly to a table. RLP, being smarter than the table, led a trip to Harbor Freight for some clamps. RLP has made some good and some bad purchases at Harbor Freight. The clamps were a bad purchase. We were able to successfully cover the table, some chairs and part of the wall with flour but fortunately did not break the table. After making the trip home, RLP figured out there must be a better way.

One of the characteristics of a good *Real Life Prepper* is that they are sometimes able to see multiple or different uses for a regular, everyday item. After returning home, RLP led another trip to Harbor Freight and this time made a good purchase. A bench grinder stand [L112] http://www.harborfreight.com/universal-bench-grinder-stand-3184.html was the first thing that went into the cart. After drilling a few bolt holes in the top, that stand is now the permanent base for the Country Living Grain Mill in the RLP family home. "Sorry about the flour mess, buddy. At least we did not break your table."

Honey is also a real LTS food. Most people believe that real honey has an infinite shelf life. RLP recommends purchasing real, unprocessed, local honey. Do not buy the blended honey from foreign countries sold at Sam's or Costco. Honey also has many other efficacious properties such as being sweeter than sugar, helps prevent local allergies, and has antibiotic properties. Some folks believe that honey should not be served to a child less than one-year old.

Beans and rice can be considered LTS foods. Properly stored, they can last a long time but do need to be preserved properly. In the pantry, white rice lasts about one year. Brown rice (because of the oil content) lasts about six months in the same environment. White rice stored in an oxygen fee environment lasts considerably longer. Lima beans have an 8-month storage life in the freezer. Dried lima beans stored in an oxygen free environment last considerably longer.

One of the first questions that comes up when a regular family decides to look at becoming a *Real Life Prepper* family is, "Hey, where can I buy that kind of long term storage food?" The RLP family did exactly the same thing. Fortunately, RLP had watched television once in his life and knew that Mormons (Latter-Day Saints or LDS) were supposed to stock up on food. They probably already knew the answer.

After a bit of internet research, RLP stumbled upon a source. The Mormon Church maintains a LTS food information site [L113] https://www.lds.org/topics/food-storage/longer-term-food-supply?lang=eng#1 that provides great and free information. Fortunately they are very gracious and are willing to share their knowledge with gentiles. They also run what RLP calls LDS canneries [L114] http://www.providentliving.org/?lang=eng around the country and most of the time, are willing to share those resources with gentiles. RLP greatly appreciates their ministry and highly recommends their high quality and high value LTS food options.

Garden
Some folks believe that if you do not have a garden and the schumer hits the fan, you are going to die. RLP recommends that you start a garden now, even if it is a modest experiment. If you have limited resources, RLP recommends you follow the advice of Mel Bartholomew in his Square Foot Gardening book [L056] http://www.amazon.com/Square-Foot-Gardening-Second-Revolutionary/dp/1591865484/ref=sr_1_1_title_1_pap?s=books&ie=UTF8&qid=1392247883&sr=1-1&keywords=square+foot+gardening.

RLP believes that the best garden is a garden of fish. A stocked pond or lake is easier to defend than a dirt garden and can be more sustainable.

Sprouts
RLP faced many problems with the RLP family garden experiments. Bugs ate the food, deer ate the food, raccoons ate the food, and all of one type of food was ready for harvest at the same time. Most importantly, it was hard to grow tomatoes in the dead of winter. How is

RLP going to maintain nutrient-rich food in the middle of winter? Sprouts became the answer. RLP highly recommends the advice and products available from the Sprout People [L057] http://sproutpeople.org/. Sprouts are incredibly useful and convenient. Do your research and experiment. You will thank me later.

Getting to the Food

Sometimes this can be incredibly hard. MrsRLP has some difficulty opening cans even when there is electricity available. What are we to do if the grid is down and RLP is hungry? RLP recommends the following two manual can openers

- EZ-DUZ-IT Can Opener [L058]
    - http://www.amazon.com/gp/product/B008AWCI8M/ref=oh_details_o00_s00_i03?ie=UTF8&psc=1
- Made in USA Can Opener[L059]
    - http://www.amazon.com/gp/product/B007DK6SG0/ref=oh_details_o00_s00_i01?ie=UTF8&psc=1.

Also purchase a few (read that as many) P-38 and P-51 can openers. They are available everywhere, are small, and can open virtually any metal can.

RLP recommends a manual tool made by Evriholder called the EasiTwist Jar Opener [L060] http://www.evriholder.com/EasiTwist-Jar-Opener.asp to get lids off of jars. This is particularly useful to someone with a compromised grip. The EasiTwist is available in many places, including Amazon.

So how do you get into that sealed 5-gallon bucket? You need an opener to pry off that lid that will leave your finger tips intact. RLP recommends the Linzer 5425 Plastic 5-Gallon Paint Can Opener [L058] http://www.amazon.com/gp/product/B000KKPBFE/ref=oh_details_o04_s00_i01?ie=UTF8&psc=1 available everywhere. Get more than one. You will thank me later.

Another alternative is to not actually "seal" the bucket. Use a temporary, reusable, water-tight, twist-off lid made by Baytec. They are called gamma seal lids [L059] http://www.bayteccontainers.com/gamma-seal-lids.html and are available virtually everywhere. A press fit rubber seal keeps them connected to the bucket. Use a rubber mallet. An easy twist (hand operated) threaded cap controls access to the bucket. They can be ordered color-coded and can convert several different size buckets into other types of storage containers even if they are not food-grade. Think nails, parts, etc. They are cheaper if you can buy them in bulk. The RLP family uses food grade buckets with a red gamma seal lid to store ready access red winter wheat, a white gamma seal lid to store ready access white winter wheat, and a blue gamma seal lid to store ready access sea salt.

Refrigerator Food

Yes, you can store food in a refrigerator! What a novel thought! If you lose electricity, the food in your refrigerator should be good for at least four hours if you keep the door shut. A properly sized but small generator can keep electricity supplied to your refrigerator, and freezer, for a virtually unlimited time. Make sure you know how to operate the generator and that you have all of the supplies needed. A friend of mine had the properly sized generator and enough fuel but could not even start the generator when it was needed after a tornado because he did not have any oil. Where possible, all members of your household should be trained and practiced to start and maintain the generator.

How am I going to prepare this?

Wow, RLP, this is a very good question. While MREs can be eaten readily, other things are best eaten after cooking. Are you planning on cooking inside or outside? You probably already know how to cook inside if you can keep from killing yourself from carbon monoxide poisoning. Cooking inside using alternative fuels is something best studied and practiced before it is needed.

Cooking outside is something you may not be as familiar with. You may already be using your standard propane outdoor BBQ cooker. Some of those grills can also be modified to use the natural gas you have piped into your house. A charcoal grill can get you by for a while. Be aware that cooking outside can give away the fact that you have hot food available and may not be the best thing for your operational security. In addition, a four burner, propane grill is not the easiest thing to carry on your back as you are hiking to a safe place. And the 20-pound propane tank weighs at least another 20 pounds.

RLP recommends you invest in a BioLite Camp Stove. The Biolite Camp stove [L063] http://www.biolitestove.com started out as a way to reduce the effects of cooking smoke in third-world countries (a major cause of death). This stove burns virtually any organic material you find along the trail or at camp. The "power" module fits in the stove cylinder for transport so that the entire package is about the same diameter as a three-liter soda bottle but not as tall. The power module contains rechargeable batteries. The batteries power a fan that blows directly in the fire to make it start fast and burn well. When the stove is burning, it runs the fan and generates excess electricity that you can use to charge your cell phone or other device through the USB port. You use the same USB port to keep the power module charged for kick-start purposes. Imagine not having to purchase specialized fuel containers (or have to carry them) when you go hiking. There are some accessories that I have not tried. One is a small grill top. Another is the KettlePot that I received for Christmas. But I had to buy it for myself!

MEDICAL

With the advent of the Affordable Care Act, medical care is no longer the quality it used to be nor is it affordable. However, it should be near the top of your list for real life prepping. Just as in fire protection, good health should focus on maintenance (prevention of bad health) as your top priority. If you maintain your good health, you will not waste a lot of resources trying to regain it.

First Aid Kit

Clearly you need a first aid kit. RLP has been there and has done that. Subscribing to the false principle that if small is good, then bigger must be better; RLP has invested in large business oriented kits in big plastic boxes with a great selection of first aid materials inside. The problem is that many of the supplies inside the kits are unneeded and also expire. Virtually every band aid inside each of the kits has been worthless by the time I got to it. The adhesive just gave up the ghost. And RLP never could read the fine print instruction pamphlet included in the manufacturer's kit anyway.

RLP recommends you use those kits as a guideline and construct your own kit(s). The American Red Cross [L076] http://www.redcross.org/prepare/location/home-family/get-kit/anatomy does give you a start in the right direction although RLP does not believe it is the definitive source. The RLP family has now invested in a substantial red plastic box (the type available from Lowes or Office Depot) and has stocked it to meet the needs of our family. All of your first aid needs are not going to be caused by the zombie apocalypse.

You need more than one first aid kit. You need

perhaps two or three for your house and one for each vehicle. RLP recommends you use a smaller, flexible pouch for your vehicles, not a big red plastic box. When you are aiding strangers on the road, your concerns and needs are different than when you are aiding your family in your own home.

Although you are probably not reluctant to administer cardiopulmonary resuscitation (CPR) to a family member, you may hesitate to help a bloody stranger who has been involved in a car accident. You need to protect yourself, particularly from blood pathogens. At the same time, you are called to help the needy. A balance may be reached by using a CPR shield. You can easily get them small enough to keep one or two in your vehicle first aid kit and another couple at the office. RLP highly recommends the American CPR Mini CPR Keychain [L077] https://www.americancpr.com/barrier.html or something similar because of their size and cost. RLP still prefers a better but larger alternative, the Ambu Res-Cue CPR Mask Kit available everywhere.

Medical Training

Other than proper exercise and eating right, first aid training is the best thing you can do to leverage your capability to preserve your health. Each member of your family that is capable should obtain and maintain basic first aid, CPR, and blood pathogen training. Normally the American Red Cross can provide this type of training at a pretty low cost. Do not feel that you have to be an Emergency Medical Technician (EMT) to provide real life first aid. Any good first aid training is better than no first aid training. However, EMT training can be a good idea for a large family or a neighborhood community. RLP certified as a Nationally Registered Emergency Medical Technician (NREMT) many years ago and considers it a great investment although I never practiced in the occupation.

Prescription Drugs

Many folks rely on prescription drugs to maintain their health. This can include things like blood pressure medicine, diabetes medicine, and anti-rejection drugs. They can be critical to maintaining good health in a real life situation. RLP highly recommends you do what it takes to convince your Doctor to help you maintain your health in a more reliable fashion. That can be done simply by changing your prescription from a 30-day supply to a 90-day supply. An interruption in your supply can adversely impact your life.

Other Doctors may want to put you or your family on a Statin (like Crestor) to control your high cholesterol. RLP suggests that there may be unwanted side effects and more natural ways to control high cholesterol in real life situations. RLP recommends that you at least evaluate the claims from the book, *Cholesterol Down* [L092] http://www.amazon.com/Cholesterol-Down-Simple-Weeks-Without-Prescription/dp/0307339114 before making life impacting decisions.

Antibiotics

The *Doomsday Prepper* is always looking for alternative supplies to antibiotics. The *Real Life Prepper* knows not to abuse the antibiotics but considers the implications of not having them readily available when needed. RLP recommends you develop a friendly relationship with your Doctor of choice and lay the groundwork for the prescription of antibiotics before you actually need them. The *Doomsday Prepper* has already laid in a stock of fish or other animal antibiotics to use in case a Doctor is not available or willing to prescribe what they think they need.

Whole and Natural Foods

RLP is convinced that much food and many vitamins are not good for you. Artificial sweeteners, processed foods, margarine, and Genetically Modified Organisms (GMO) may be worse then we think. In particular, RLP is against synthetic vitamins. RLP highly recommends you research whole food vitamins and discard your synthetic vitamins. One possible alternative is Vitamin Code [L078] http://www.amazon.com/gp/product/B00323NW5C/ref=oh_details_o05_s00_i00?ie=UTF8&psc=1.

RLP believes that much of the current anti-gluten campaign is based more on how bad processed white flour is for you rather than how natural gluten in whole wheat impacts your health. RLP is definitely not a gluten expert. The anti-gluten group may have very valid arguments. My sense is that many of their arguments are as emotional as scientific. It comes across with the same logic as the global warming crowd. If you would like to pursue more information about gluten, you may want to start out with the website Against All Grain [L093] http://againstallgrain.com/ or do some research about the Paleo Diet [L094] http://thepaleodiet.com/

As little as RLP knows about gluten, he knows less about essential oils and herbs. However, there have been demonstrated significant recent promises in managing good health through the use of essential oils and natural herbs without the necessity of artificial drugs and synthetics marketed by the drug industry. You may want to begin your own research at an Essential Oils website [L095] http://www.aromaweb.com/essentialoils/default.asp and a Natural Herbs Guide [L096] http://www.naturalherbsguide.com/index.html

RLP has never been accused of being politically

correct. Sometimes he just cannot help himself. He cannot just leave it alone. The global warming crowd seems to have left real science and intellectual honesty behind a while ago to pursue political goals. Please pursue your own goals with wisdom.

Trauma Gear

In a real life situation, do you actually think you need some trauma gear in your house, or on the range, without having the proper training to use it? Can you even get the trauma gear as a *Real Life Prepper*? The answer to both of these questions is a resounding, "Yes!" Do not believe the written materials that tell you a Doctor's prescription is required to purchase the gear you need. It is much better to have a neighbor or friend with the proper training show up to save your family's life with your pre-positioned gear than to have them drive back to the hospital to get what they need. The RLP family has even carried some of this type of gear on foreign mission trips rather than rely of questionable supplies in other countries.

Here RLP will list some trauma gear you may want to pre-position.

- 10cc syringe (without needle) [L079]
    - http://www.amazon.com/gp/product/B0 00O0BT2O/ref=oh_details_o04_s00_i0 0?ie=UTF8&psc=1
- Stainless steel blunt needle [L080]
    - http://www.amazon.com/gp/product/B0 013J403U/ref=oh_details_o03_s00_i00? ie=UTF8&psc=1
- Medical scissors [L081]
    - http://www.amazon.com/gp/product/B0 02WJHE7E/ref=oh_details_o06_s01_i0 2?ie=UTF8&psc=1
- Oral airway kit [L082]

- o http://www.amazon.com/gp/product/B0
  015E2FDK/ref=oh_details_o07_s00_i0
  0?ie=UTF8&psc=1
- Manual resuscitator [L083]
  - o http://www.amazon.com/gp/product/B0
    00WLG43Y/ref=oh_details_o07_s00_i0
    1?ie=UTF8&psc=1
- Nasopharyngeal Airway [L084]
  - o http://www.amazon.com/gp/product/B0
    03950R2E/ref=oh_details_o07_s00_i02
    ?ie=UTF8&psc=1
- Chest Seal [L085]
  - o http://www.amazon.com/gp/product/B0
    03VSRO1Q/ref=oh_details_o07_s00_i0
    3?ie=UTF8&psc=1
- QuikClot Sport Advanced Clotting Sponge
  [L086]
  - o http://www.amazon.com/Quikclot-
    Advanced-Clotting-Bleeding-
    Package/dp/B001BCNTHC/ref=sr_1_5?
    s=hpc&ie=UTF8&qid=1392690169&sr
    =1-5&keywords=celox
  - o RLP highly recommends you stay away
    from the powdered type of QuikClot or
    Celox. Stay with a sponge or a Z-fold.
- QuikClot Combat Gauze (Z-Fold) [L087]
  - o http://www.amazon.com/gp/product/B0
    01E1CLTC/ref=oh_details_o06_s00_i0
    0?ie=UTF8&psc=1
- Israeli Battle Dressing [L088]
  - o http://www.amazon.com/THE-
    EMERGENCY-BANDAGE-Dressing-
    Compression/dp/B00CBX90FK/ref=sr_
    1_1?s=sporting-
    goods&ie=UTF8&qid=1392690735&sr
    =1-1&keywords=israeli+bandage
- SWAT-T Stretch-Wrap-and-Tuck Tourniquet
  [L138]
  - o http://www.swattourniquet.com/

You can nicely pre-position your trauma gear in

a bag similar to the Medical Rescue Response Bag
[L089]

- http://www.amazon.com/gp/product/B000I672G
  6/ref=oh_details_o06_s00_i01?ie=UTF8&psc=1

Whenever RLP is teaching on the range, the
bright orange trauma bag is highly visible and available
to all students.

Dental

Whereas bad general health can kill you, bad
dental health can make you feel miserable while you are
still alive. Sometimes you need dental intervention
before it is available from your own Dentist. As a *Real
Life Prepper*, you can prepare for that type of
contingency. RLP recommends you pre-position an
emergency dental kit [L090]

- http://www.amazon.com/gp/product/B001MA31
  6C/ref=oh_details_o08_s00_i00?ie=UTF8&psc
  =1

and a filling repair kit [L091].

- http://www.amazon.com/gp/product/B002WTC
  K50/ref=oh_details_o00_s00_i00?ie=UTF8&ps
  c=1

These kits are small enough and cheap enough to carry
in your regular hiking pack.

Fighting dental issues is certainly not as easy as
maintaining dental health in the first place. Follow your
Dentist's instructions. Get your semi-annual checkups.
RLP was raised when Dentists were teaching you to
brush three times a day and floss after one brushing. The
new school of thought considers flossing much more
important than brushing and recommends flossing
before brushing. I am sure that the Dentists of the world
are glad that RLP agrees with the new school of thought.

Many Dentists are also now recommending alcohol-free mouthwash. The jury is still out on this issue and some folks say that this type of mouthwash stains your teeth. RLP will be sure to inform the Dentists of the world when he makes his determination.

Eye Glasses

RLP recommends you keep your last, old pair of glasses when you get new ones. A little vision and eye protection is better than none. And from personal experience, RLP recommends you invest in several self-contained eye glass repair kits. Many are smaller than a ballpoint pen and contain the right size screw drivers and mixed screws. One suggestion is [L132]

- http://www.causa.com/store/catalog.asp?item=3721&lang=en&category_id=126

sold just about everywhere.

SECURITY

Whether you know it or not, this aspect of preparation is critical. It does not matter if you are *Doomsday Prepper* or a *Real Life Prepper*. It does not matter if you are a prepper at all. You are responsible for your own security. The government is not responsible for your personal security and sometimes they are not as responsive as they could be or as you want them to be. And sometimes they are more responsive then they need to be.

Here are some Clint Smith quotations that might help you in your thinking. Clint Smith is an ex-Marine (although some folks say, "Once a Marine, always a Marine.") and founder of Thunder Ranch.

"You cannot save the planet. You may be able to save yourself and your family."

"I carry a gun because a cop is too heavy."

"When seconds count, the cops are just minutes away."

And here is a quote from the author of *Real Life Prepper.*

"If you act like a sheep, you will be eaten by wolves."

You do not have to own or carry a gun to have some security. When the *Doomsday Prepper* thinks about survival, his mind naturally drifts to the mutant ninja biker zombies or the zombie apocalypse and their inevitable attacks on all that you hold dear. RLP recommends that you take your security seriously but not go off the deep end. The best thing you can do if you are just starting out is to not cooperate with the bad guys. Refuse to be a victim. The National Rifle Association (NRA) offers a four-hour, non-firearm

course with that title, *"Refuse To Be A Victim."* [L015]
http://refuse.nra.org/. Although initially designed for
women, RTBAV is a great course for your entire family.
You can apply the lessons learned in this seminar to
your everyday (real) life and then expand the principles
into your preparation activities.

Criminals are not that interested in bothering
someone who is going to give them trouble. They are
interested in easy targets. You do not want to make
yourself or your home an easy target. Do not let your
neighbor read *Real Life Prepper* or attend the RTBAV
seminar. The criminals will be so interested in your
neighbor they will not bother you.

Mindset

RLP believes your best defense is between your
ears. Your mindset determines the way you look and the
way you act. If you feel confident, you will look
confident. If you are determined to survive, you stand a
better chance of survival. Many FBI and other studies
come to the same conclusion. The potential victim who
resists and fights back stands a much better chance than
the passive, compliant victim of not getting injured,
raped, or killed. Fight back, scream, and never give up.

During my military days, we were trained to act
passive if taken hostage in an airplane. Comply and let
the professionals handle the negotiations when you land.
Ask yourself if there was any difference in the
consequences for the three airplanes taken over by the
9/11 terrorists. Granted, the Pennsylvania airplane still
crashed but those heroes potentially saved many lives.
Box cutters or not, with the proper mindset, the terrorists
will not be able to stand against regular, unarmed
passengers.

Be aware of your surroundings. Be conscious of
where you are, where other people are, and what is

going on around you. Call me paranoid, but there are things I do that I can heartily recommend to you. That way, I will not be the only paranoid person around. The RLP family likes to go to movies. Every time we sit down, I ask MrsRLP the same question. Without looking around, where are the exits? When we go into a restaurant, I look for the exits and always sit facing the entrance rather than with my back to it. When we park our car, we always try to park where it is visible and under a street light, even if it is a few more steps. This is not being paranoid, it is just being smart.

Locks

Please add reasonable locks on your doors and windows. Lock your home, including your garage door, even when you are home – particularly when you are home. Examine your home from the outside through the eyes of a criminal. If you use a deadbolt for your front door, can someone bust the glass in the door, reach in, and twist the lock open? In that case, you may want to use a lock that is keyed on both sides. Does everyone in your household have access to that key so they can evacuate the building if there is a need?

Lights

Criminals will also not like your house if it is lit up. Many homes come with outside floodlights on the corners. They are normally switch-activated. These flood lights can be easily swapped out with motion-activated lights that operate only when it is dark outside. During a power failure, these lights will not operate. Solar-charged, battery operated, LED lights can be used in addition to, or in place of, your regular AC powered flood lights.

There are two other locations where you may want to place a motion-activated flood light. The first place is under your second-story deck where you keep your trash cans. Houses that are constructed in this fashion usually have a basement or garage entry into your house from under the deck. The second place may seem unusual but is really handy. The RLP basement garage is dark. Normally you turn on the overhead light when you enter the garage in the morning. Then you have to remember to turn it off. How do you do that after you are in your car? We installed a motion-activated flood light in the ceiling of the basement garage. The light comes on automatically when it senses movement (but only when it is dark outside) and times itself out when the movement stops. No more having to remember to turn the light off! And I feel comfortable that no one is lurking in my dark garage.

Automatic timers, some with a built-in random function, can be used to activate lamps and other lights in your house regardless of whether or not you are home. This simulated activity can serve to discourage bad guys from breaking into your house. They never know if you are home or not.

Of course you want to be able to see around your house if the power goes out. Or do you? You know your house better than anyone else. You know which step creaks and where the loose floor boards are. You know where the doorknobs and locks are. You know which way every door swings. You may find it a tactical advantage to not be seen and to not turn on the lights. You can operate in your dark house a lot easier than a bad guy.

But what if you did want to have light if the power went out? Think about an automatic flashlight. One such example is the Eco-i-Lite [L016] http://www.capstoneindustries.com/index.php/products/eco-i-lite-6led-power-failure-light/. This LED flashlight sets in a charging base that is always plugged into your wall socket. The base can be configured as a nightlight or to always be dark. When the power goes out or the flashlight is simply pulled out of the base, it comes on. It is very simple and convenient. The flashlight button also turns it on/off or into a flasher.

What about your night vision? Remember folks telling you to use red light to protect your night vision? They lied. Or at least they exaggerated. The red light solution came from the early days of photography because photo-sensitive paper was less sensitive to red light. Red light works but a blue-green light may work better. A cheap solution is a string of blue or red LED lights, like Christmas lights. They come in different lengths. Search the internet for rope lights. While many use 110v AC power with a rectifier, others run directly off of a 12v power supply like a car battery.

Alarms

A certain percentage of our population uses, and swears by, a professional burglar alarm system. It has value and does serve a purpose. But it also has a cost. There is an initial installation cost and a periodic, usually monthly, monitoring charge. RLP does not recommend the use of a professional burglar alarm system unless you are going to use a professional monitoring service. A professional system is not useful unless it is used and should be activated even when you are home. You need to operate within the parameters needed to not set off false alarms and remember to always set it.

There is an alternative that works almost as well. Remember the criminal that is not interested in something that is going to give them trouble? If you were a criminal and all other things were equal, would you break into a home with a burglar alarm system or a home that did not have one? How does a criminal know that you have a burglar alarm installed? Of course, they see the stickers and the sign. The stickers and the signs are available on eBay and on Amazon. How is the criminal to know you are lying? They probably will not sue you for cheating.

Another way to cheat is to have a very big dog food bowl and water bowl on you back porch. How will the bad guy know that the biggest dog you have is a parakeet?

There are circumstances and situations where you want to have an alarm. If you have an out-building like a storage shed or barn, you might want to put a local alarm on the doors and windows. If you have a long or non-visible driveway, you might install a driveway alarm. The expensive kind is embedded in the driveway and detects a vehicle driving over the detector. It does not detect a person walking down your driveway. A "driveway alarm" is battery powered and detects movement, including cars, people, and cats, within its detector range. RLP recommends something like the 200-foot range driveway alarm made by Bunker Hill Security. It is available on eBay, on Amazon, and from Harbor Freight.

Non-Firearm Firearms

For various reasons, you may elect not to employ a firearm as part of your security strategy. In fact, the municipality where you live may restrict your 2nd amendment rights. There are alternatives here also. Flare guns and flares themselves are usually not banned. The Coast Guard may even insist you carry a signaling device such as a flare gun when on a boat. You can have the flare gun in your home or under the seat of your car to use for signaling purposes. If I was a bad guy, I would not want to be signaled with a 12 gauge flare. RLP recommends the Orion Alerter Basic [L017] http://www.orionsignals.com/applications/marine/produ ct/76.html. Kennesaw Cannon also sells a sub caliber device [L018] http://kennesawcannon.com/subcaliberdevice.php that slips into the correct size flare gun and fires 22LR or .45 Long Colt and 410 shotgun shells. Mere possession of a suitable flare gun and the sub caliber device can be construed as having a firearm so make sure you check the regulations.

Non-Firearm Defense

Although you may not be trained in the use of a defensive baton, anyone can swing a stick at a mad dog. A collapsible baton is only about 9-12 inches long and effortlessly extends to two-three feet long. If I was a mad dog or a bad guy, I would think twice before I did something serious against somebody with a baton in their hand. You can find these on eBay or Amazon. Make sure you read the reviews and know local laws. Weighing about three pounds, they fit perfectly in your briefcase or your GHB.

Now for you *Walking Dead* or *Arrow* fans. Another option is a crossbow, good out to about 40 yards. It is not as easy as depicted, nor is it fast, to cock the bow. However, there are some advantages. You do not need a license to purchase or operate a crossbow. There are normally no known city limit restrictions on the operation of the crossbow. You can recover and reuse the arrows or bolts. Firing the crossbow is relatively quiet. Most importantly, it looks awesome.

The crossbow also has some disadvantages. Most of them are not small and it is not easy to carry one concealed inside your waistband. You should only leave the crossbow cocked for about four hours at a time. You need to pay close attention to your maintenance. For instance, you need to apply string lube about every five times you fire. The broad-heads (arrow heads) are really razor blades and require great care in handling. You cannot easily unload a crossbow but rather must safely discharge it to unload.

For a larger crossbow, RLP recommends something like the Barnett Quad 400. It has a 150-pound draw weight. To cock this by hand, you need to really want it. This may be mitigated by the use of a rope cocking device. Better yet, an optional crank can take the effort required down to 17 pounds. The arrows (bolts) are 22-inches long.

Slingshots have come a long way since the late 1800s. Many, even with a wrist support, fold up into a small package. They can propel a marble or steel ball fast enough to deter a dog, a person, or even convince a squirrel to join you for dinner. Some high tech, sophisticated slingshots have a light mount and even a whisker biscuit so that you can fire arrows. RLP recommends the Survival Slingshot [L024] http://www.survivalslingshot.com. These are not toys.

Pepper spray and tear gas are other alternatives. If you take the RTBAV seminar, they will even demonstrate pepper spray. Warning, do not sit in the front row. Sorry to get you excited. They only demonstrate a dummy spray container so you can see the range. Do your research before you decide to carry pepper spray or tear gas.

A Taser or stun gun is another option. Although they can be effective, RLP does not recommend you rely on their use. We do not want you to get close enough to employ a taser.

Restraints

There may come a time when you are required to detain or restrain a person. For instance, a neighborhood drunk breaks into your home. You are able to stop them and you call 911. The police are 25 minutes out. Do you feel comfortable holding a gun on them for the next 25 minutes? They may be drunk enough to not care about the gun and you may not want to do them serious harm. How can you protect yourself and keep them from harming themselves? The answer is to restrain them. Of course, you could always go out, find a rope, and hog tie them. Or more realistically, restrain them in an easier and safer fashion.

Thick wire ties, sometimes referred to as zip ties or self-locking cable ties are one option. Safariland makes some designed for cuff restraints with a 300 pound tensile strength. [L023] http://www.defensedevices.com/hiatt-cable-restraints.html. These specially designed ties have rounded edges and are pick resistant. Normal zip ties have a 50-75 pound tensile strength.

Another option is handcuffs. No, you do not need a license. Yes, they are available on eBay or Amazon. In most cases, the handcuff keys are universal. Even if you do not get handcuffs, you might think about being prepared by purchasing some of these universal handcuff keys. Some enterprising folks even sell a plastic handcuff key that looks like a regular zipper pull. They work. Do not ask me how I know. Regardless, get someone to show you how to use them. There are two basic types of handcuffs, hinged and chained. RLP recommends you purchase the hinged type. It helps prevent anyone from getting pinched. And they should be made of metal, not leather or fur.

Safes

Here are the two rules about safes. One, you need a safe. Two, the one you buy will be too small. RLP recommends you explore Liberty Safes [L040] http://www.libertysafe.com/. Even if you end up not buying a Liberty safe, you can learn a lot from their website. Be aware that safes are heavy. A delivery service will charge you about $80 to deliver a 900 pound safe. They may charge you an additional $50 per step if they have to use stairs.

The Liberty type of traditional safe is big and bad. Pay attention to the fire rating. If you store firearms, cash, photographs, or papers in the safe, you want it to protect them from heat, flames, and smoke. Consider the purpose of your safe. Like many other choices, this one is driven by the purpose. There are two types of access into this traditional safe type. The old type of lock is a UL listed mechanical lock. The traditional combination lock is considerably slower than an electronic lock but does not rely on batteries or electronic circuitry. The new type of lock is a UL listed electronic lock with a touchpad. They offer very quick access and enable the owner to change the combination. The mechanical lock requires a locksmith to change the combination. Some of these electronic locks can be configured to alternatively open with a fingerprint (biometric).

Regardless of the type of lock, the placement of the safe is critical to its security. RLP recommends you position the safe in a corner of your basement adjacent to concrete walls and that you bolt it down from the inside to the concrete floor. Normally a burglar needs to lay the safe on its back to attempt crow barring the door open.

We all want the speed and convenience of the touchpad but some of us want the higher reliability of the mechanical lock. The answer may be found in the simplex mechanical lock. The simplex lock is mechanical but only comes with five pushbuttons, numbered one through five. The lock is quick to operate, secure, not subject to electronic or power issues, and can be operated in the dark – by feel. The combination can be changed by the owner.

One vendor of lockboxes and vaults that use the simplex lock is V-Line [L041] http://vlineind.com/Default.php . V-Line makes a great vault that mounts in between studs and is only the depth of a 2x4 (your wall). It is perfect to mount in a master bedroom closet behind the door. V-Line makes an array of vaults and security cases that may meet your needs.

Another vendor using simplex locks is Fas1 [L042] http://fas1safe.com . I have seen this safe mounted in a console of a truck. I have also seen it mounted in the floor of a bedroom below a false HVAC supply register.

Firearms

We eventually always get around to firearms when we talk about security. Defending yourself and your family is a God-given right; it is a right not granted by, but can only be restricted by, governments. Whether you own, carry, or use a firearm should be a choice you make based on your own personal circumstances.

Firearms are acquired for a variety of reasons. Some folks just want to collect them. Some folks want to use them to hunt. Some folks just want them so they can exercise their 2nd amendment rights. And some folks want to have them to help provide for their own security. Regardless of the reason for the acquisition, possession carries with it some responsibilities. Firearms are tools. But they are tools that can do harm. A table saw is a tool that can also do harm. Both of them can wreak havoc when used improperly. RLP recommends that you have the proper training regardless of the purpose of your firearms. A firearm and a table saw both must be controlled so that they are not misused.

Assuming you have the necessary training, a firearm can greatly enhance your personal, family, and home security. Probably the best firearm you can have to provide the minimal level of home security is a shotgun. Just because Vice-President Biden suggested it once does not make it wrong. RLP recommends either the Mossberg 590A1 (not the 500) or the Remington 870 shotgun for home defense.

RLP is a certified NRA firearms instructor. We have attended a large number of training classes, observed many fellow students, taught a large number of folks, and observed many of our own students. The question we have seen and heard asked most frequently is, "What kind of firearm should I buy?" While the answer depends primarily on what the purpose of the firearm is, the purpose we are discussing here is personal defense. The answer is almost self-evident from the many observations. We want a gun that goes bang when we want it to go bang. We also want it to not go bang when we do not intend it to go bang. The answer for a highly trained, experienced, and proficient gun owner may be different than for a beginner or for someone who does not want to become a gun aficionado. For someone who is just starting out, RLP recommends a G19 or G17 Glock chambered in 9mm Parabellum or a G23 or G22 Glock chambered in .40 S&W.

So what kind of holster should you get? RLP used to normally carry concealed using a Blackhawk Serpa. The Serpa is banned at Front Sight so we needed a new holster when we went to that training. The Blade-Tech Eclipse OWB was cheap enough to use for a four-day class so we got one for a G17 and one for a G23. Both guns fit the same and feel the same. There is no sense that the Glock(s) would fall out of the holster (a great fear of mine), even when running. The holster is designed to go on belt loops - BUY A GUN BELT - and can be a little awkward when positioning. We put the belt through the back holster loop, a pants loop, then the forward holster loop. It makes it much more secure but limits the travel around the circumference of your waist. It can only go back and forth until the holster loop meets the pants loop. A belt loop holster is not as convenient as a paddle holster. However, the holster conforms well to the curvature of my body and lies pretty flat making it much easier to conceal. The kydex/plastic at the top between my body and the gun was uncomfortable at first and sort of stuck in my ribs when I twisted or sat down wrong. After a while (when I became used to it), the sensation became unnoticeable. It is designed to protect your skin and the firearm from sweat. I never adjusted the tensioning screw and the tension did not appear to change. After about 1,000 draws and re-insertions for each holster in four days, there is just a barely detectable wear mark on the holster (it may even rub off with my fingers) and none on the gun. The only problem with the holster is based on the style - you have to take your belt off to mount or un-mount the holster. I should have bought the Blade-Tech before the Serpa.

Carrying a firearm, either open-carry or concealed, carries with it an additional set of concerns. If you are not willing to use that firearm to do harm to someone who is trying to do you harm, you have no reason to be carrying it. Training with this firearm is even more important than training with your home defense shotgun. If you do end up using that firearm for defense, even if you are completely in the right, your life will change forever. You need to prepare yourself for those changes.

Other Firearm Preparations without a Firearm

The *Real Life Prepper* may decide they do not want to own or carry a firearm. That is a personal decision but RLP has some recommendations anyway. Concealed carry is primarily regulated by the States. Alabama is an open carry state. Anyone (not otherwise prohibited) can drive a car around with a firearm on their dashboard (not recommended by RLP) as long as it is visible. However, if the firearm is under the seat, under your jacket, or in the glove compartment, it is concealed. Unless you have a concealed carry permit, you are violating Alabama state law. Recently a friend of mine (with a concealed carry permit) left their firearm under the seat of another friend's (with no concealed carry permit) car seat just for a few hours. Although the firearm was always secure, the second friend could have been in legal trouble without even knowing it.

In most places there is no requirement to even own a firearm to obtain a concealed carry permit. RLP recommends every *Real Life Prepper* apply for and obtain a concealed carry permit. One never knows if you might change your mind, the state becomes more draconian, or if someone makes a simple administrative error.

RLP highly recommends you train for and obtain a concealed carry permit from Utah or Florida. Both states issue permits to non-residents and they are fully legal and recognized by 30 plus other states. Ownership and possession of a firearm is not a prerequisite to the permit.

Liability Insurance

Remember the Zimmerman/Martin incident? Regardless of which side, if any, you support, Zimmerman had/has some legal issues. You may be in similar situation someday and RLP wants you to be prepared. It does not matter whether or not you are totally innocent and totally justified. You will face some issues. What we are asking you to do is to consider this in advance and make some sort of decision to take or not take some protective measures.

RLP highly recommends you consider some type of liability insurance to protect your freedom and assets. Normal home or umbrella liability insurance does not cover self-defense use of a firearm because it is intentional, not an accident. We are not attorneys, accountants, or insurance salesmen. We do not provide legal, accounting, or insurance advice. RLP is just a voice crying out in the wilderness for you to consider your actions and their consequences. You make your own choices and decisions.

There are several organizations and companies that provide the type of insurance we are talking about. There are probably others we do not know about. We do know about the United States Concealed Carry Association (USCCA). You can reach them at [L019] http://www.uscca.org. In addition to publishing a very nice magazine, they offer three different levels of insurance that pay "after the fact." We also know about Second Call Defense (SCD). SCD offers five different levels of insurance, includes your spouse for a very small fee, and pays "as you need it." SCD is associated with the NRA and Lockton Insurance. You can reach SCD at [L020] http://www.secondcalldefense.org/. RLP highly recommends SCD.

If you make a decision to take some protective measures and to go with SCD, please indicate the *Real Life Prepper* "Recruiter ID" of 20233 so that we can get some credit. This is not a requirement. We just want you to make the best decision you can for you and for your family. So please evaluate your own circumstances carefully and do what is best for you. But please decide to do or not do something in advance.

Firearms and Security Training

Firearms and security training is probably the most critical element of your security preparations. It also provides the most bang for your buck. Do yourself a favor and at least send your entire family to a RTBAV seminar. NRA instructors teach a series of firearms courses at different levels. Even if you had other training such as in boot camp, it is to your advantage to take some of these courses. You can search for a course near you or find descriptions of the courses at [L021] http://www.nrainstructors.org/searchcourse.aspx Many of the pistol instructors provide a variety of firearms for you to try before you make a decision on which firearm to purchase. RLP recommends the eight-hour "NRA Basic Pistol Shooting Course" as your first course.

Beg, borrow, or steal a rifle! Appleseed is a fantastic opportunity and a great deal. Project Appleseed is conducted by The Revolutionary War Veterans Association and teaches about the founding of our country while giving some of the best rifle marksmanship training you can buy at any price. Find more about Project Appleseed at [L022] http://www.appleseedinfo.org/.

Please do not tell Ignatius (he could probably easily kick my rear-end) but he can get on my nerves as a salesman. However, he has what I believe to be the finest self-defense gun training program in existence. Front Sight Firearms Training Institute is in one word, fabulous. Find out about Front Sight at [L023] http://www.frontsight.com/. RLP was impressed from the second we first saw the primary campus in Nevada. We were only more impressed as we met the instructors, saw the facilities, and took some courses. And speaking of sales, look carefully for deals and you might get off fairly cheaply for your first course. I can almost guarantee that you will want to go back.

Emergencies and Duress

Imagine a scenario where your spouse is at home and you are at the bookstore getting RLP to autograph your copy of this book. We learn that all of the phone lines are down and in thirty minutes, a terrorist attack is going to take out half of your city. This includes your child's school and your house. RLP, being the nice guy he is, volunteers to evacuate your spouse while you evacuate your child. A few minutes later, RLP knocks on your front door and tells your spouse they have four minutes to get in the truck with a person they have never seen before and evacuate, possibly never to return. Would your spouse get in my truck?

RLP recommends that you discuss this type of scenario in advance with your spouse and children. Discuss scenarios perhaps not as far-fetched as the earlier paragraph, but you can probably make some applications. How can your spouse be assured that the message or instructions being delivered actually came from you and that the messenger should be trusted? We recommend you come up with a secret phrase that only you and your spouse or you and your children know. Three words should be sufficient. Make it easy to remember, easy to use, and not easy to compromise. Perhaps two phrases might be better. One that means, "Trust this messenger." and the other that means, "I am under duress. Get help." Here is an example. If your name is "Sam," your trust phrase might be "salami and meatballs." Here it is in use. "Tell my husband that I know he wanted fried chicken for dinner but we are going to have salami and meatballs with our spaghetti." Use a totally different phrase, one that cannot be easily mixed up, for your duress code. This may be too "cloak and dagger" for you, but you also might be surprised how handy it could be in an emergency. We recommend you not use "salami and meatballs" for your trust phrase.

PER SEC and OP SEC

Personal security can be enhanced by taking some of the steps laid out in this chapter. Your best bet is to take some training classes as outlined here and in the Skills and Training chapter. Operational security is easier lost than obtained. Loose lips sink ships. Your mouth is what is going to get you in trouble here. As a brand new prepper, you will probably get the disease. You will be tempted to recruit others because you have seen the light and you feel compelled to share it. Many of the folks you talk to will think you are totally weird. I speak from experience. Others will remember you. All will think the same thing and some will even speak it out loud. "I do not have to do anything. If something happens, we will just come over to your house." Let me let you down easily. You cannot survive alone but you cannot feed the world.

What has been seen cannot be unseen. RLP recommends that you keep your most intimate secrets very close to your chest. There is no reason to just show off your long term storage of food, your ammunition stockpile, or your vast array of weapons. Build a level of trust with folks before you spill your guts. Whatever you do, be careful of the internet.

Junk Mail

All junk mail is not really harmless. If you are like many other normal folks, you get unsolicited credit card and refinance applications in your mail. Usually your name, address, and a special code are printed on the application. You are probably already approved. All that you need to activate the financial transaction is to submit the paperwork or call it in. If you simply trash your junk mail, you make yourself more vulnerable to identity and financial theft. Do yourself another favor. Get a cross-cut shredder and shred anything like that with your name or the code printed on it.

REAL MONEY: A FABLE

Money can be a touchy subject so I thought I might touch on what money really is through the telling of a fable. Money is a medium used to transfer value from one person to another. In times past, folks would use large stones, beads, seashells, or things like gold to represent a certain amount of value. Today, we primarily use electronic means to represent something else (paper money) that in turn represents something else (value).

Imagine wanting to buy a loaf of bread. If the medium of exchange was a six foot diameter stone wheel with a hole in it, we might have a little trouble carrying six of them in our pocket to walk to the store. Perhaps we might use something else a little smaller as a medium of exchange. How about gold? Okay, we dig six pounds of gold out of the ground and carry it in our right front pants pocket. What happens if it wears a hole in our pocket and drops to the ground as we are attending the Saturday night barn dance and we do not notice it? Or what happens if a robber sees that bulge in our pocket and takes the gold by force? Perhaps we could find somebody with a big safe who, for a fee, will keep the gold secure until we need it.

That is a great idea. I found someone who will do that for me. She already does it for a bunch of folks. I take my six pounds of gold to my buddy, Sheila, who locks it up in the safe. In turn, she hands me a slip of paper certifying that I have six pounds of gold in the safe (minus her security fee, of course). The paper "gold certificate" does not wear a hole in my pants and I can easily conceal it from robbers. Alas, I still need that loaf of bread. When my kids get hungry, I make a trip to Sheila. I give her my gold certificate and she opens her safe then hands me my six pounds of gold. I walk with the load to my baker, Bob, and get my loaf of bread. On my way back to my buddy and her safe with the left over gold, I have another idea. I can get Sheila to issue me one gold certificate for every pound of gold and I would not have to exchange the big certificate for all six pounds of gold. She agrees. In fact, I negotiate her safeguarding my silver, too. Sheila then issues me silver certificates that all say, "Payable to the bearer on demand – one pound of silver."

Since I am an idea man, I am always trying to think of ways to save me work and effort. Just like clockwork, my kids get hungry again. I need another loaf of bread. But it is a long walk to Sheila's and that gold is heavy. I thought I would try something with Bob. I tell Bob about Sheila and her safe. Bob knows Sheila; they used to be next door neighbors. Bob trusts Sheila. I convince Bob to accept my silver certificate instead of the real thing. It is a lot easier to handle than the pound of silver. Bob can always get the physical silver later if he needs it to buy wheat or sugar. After all, it does say, "Payable to the bearer on demand – one pound of silver" and it has Sheila's signature on it. I give Bob my slip of paper (the silver certificate) and Bob gives me the bread. Everyone is happy, particularly my kids. It would be even better if Bob can convince Fred, the farmer, to take the silver certificate instead of real silver in exchange for a bushel of hard red winter wheat.

By the end of the next week, Sheila's safe is full of my gold and silver, Bob's gold and silver, Fred's gold and silver, and her own gold and silver. Larry comes into Sheila's storefront to borrow some gold (for a fee of course) from Sheila to buy some cable for a job he has to do where the homeowner will not pay in advance. He needs to borrow 14 pounds of gold. Sheila opens the safe, takes out Fred's gold and silver, takes out Bob's gold and silver, and takes out my gold and silver to reach her own bag of gold that is setting on the bottom. Unfortunately she only has ten pounds of gold and turns down poor Larry.

Things are going along very smoothly with the silver certificates. I, along with Bob and Fred, and a dozen or so others are now using them for our regular commerce. We are very happy. Sheila, on the other hand, is getting frustrated. There is all of our gold and silver setting in her vault, unused. Hardly anyone ever comes back to her to actually exchange their certificates back into physical gold and silver. She does not have enough of her own gold and silver to lend out. She is making some money safeguarding our gold and silver but she could be making more money if she had more to lend. Then the light bulb that continually hovers over her head lights up. If she "borrowed" just 10% of the gold and silver that Bob and Fred and others had deposited in her vault for safe keeping, she could have access to more gold, lend Larry what he needed, and most importantly, she could make more money. If Bob came in to exchange a certificate for physical gold and silver, there is more than enough in the vault to cover him.

Still not satisfied with how much money she is making, Sheila increases her "borrowing" from 10% to 50% and eventually settles on 95%. If she had 100 pounds of gold deposited in her vault, she would only have to keep five pounds available and could lend the other 95. Some folks might think that her "borrowing" really means "stealing." To offset her guilty feelings, she decides to pay folks a nominal fee for protecting their gold and silver rather than charge them to safeguard it. Everything is going to work out fine. Unless, of course, if Bob and Fred and others all decide to exchange their certificates for physical gold and silver at the same time.

With not having to work anymore for her own

income, Sheila has time to think. She wonders what money really is and what makes it money. It could not be value alone. Why choose gold and silver? A chicken has value. But she does not have 100 chickens living in her vault. Why did Bob and Fred, and now Larry, decide to deposit gold and silver in her vault? Sheila decides to come up with her own rules for what attributes something has to have to be considered money.

Sheila came up with seven attributes.

1. Money has to be recognizable and have a long history of acceptance. A chicken is recognizable, so is gold and silver. And who does not like fried chicken – except the chicken?
2. Money has to be able to be split up or divisible. A loaf of bread does not cost the same as a spool of cable. You can split up gold and silver. It is much harder to split up a chicken and exchange a bloody wing for a loaf of bread. Besides, the chicken does not like it.
3. Money has to be durable and retain its value. If gold or silver is locked up in Sheila's vault for a year while she is on vacation, it will still be gold and silver when she gets back. Not so much for the chicken. Loneliness was not what killed it.
4. Money has to be consistent and hard to counterfeit. Sheila remembered a time when she went to a flea market and some farmer tried to pass off a Pug (with feathers glued all over it) as a chicken. No one was fooled by that one. And then there was that time when the local Publix had a sale on tomato paste. They were selling 24 cans for a chicken. Sheila brought in a big, fat hen and walked away with a case. Patsy, her neighbor, tried to get some tomato paste for a half-dead parakeet. No deal there. Gold and silver mostly look like gold and silver. And an ounce of pure gold is an ounce of pure gold.
5. Money has to have some intrinsic value; it has to be worth something on its own. Gold and silver can be used for jewelry or electrical

contacts. You can eat a chicken. Once again, the chicken does not like that.

6. Money has to be convenient. Sheila once tried to carry a flock of chickens around in her purse. But during the movie, every time the screen lit up, one of the roosters crowed like it was sunrise. She was asked to leave. Gold and silver both seem to be really convenient.

7. Lastly, money has to be limited in quantity, a little hard to get, or rare. One of Sheila's early boyfriends, Sandy, tried to pass off sand as money. It was everywhere in unlimited quantities. Everyone was rich! That did not work. And as for chickens, all you need is a rooster, a willing chicken, and some bugs or corn. They are everywhere. It is a lot harder to dig gold and silver out of the ground. And there is only so much of it.

Sheila was pretty proud of herself. As long as those certificates continued to represent real money, everyone prospered – even with her "borrowing." Of course, she recognized that those certificates were not real money. But there was real money to back them up, as long as no one looked in her vault.

Soon the word started to spread. It was really convenient to use those certificates to conduct commerce. In fact, Susie (Sheila's cousin with her own vault in the next town) started doing the same thing. When someone in Sheila's town wanted to transact business with someone in Susie's town, it was still cumbersome. Fred would go to Sheila and exchange a Sheila-certificate for a pound of gold. He would then take the pound of gold to Susie and get a Susie-certificate. The Susie-certificate was used to buy some barbed wire to keep Fred's cows in the field where he wanted them to stay.

There was at least one more problem. Folks

wanted to transact business of smaller value than either Sheila's or Susie's certificates represented. The certificates had to be divisible. Sheila remembered her rules of real money. Real money has to be divisible. Once again her light bulb lit up. She got Mike, a metal worker, to make some coins out of her gold and silver. Folks exchanged some of their certificates that represented a pound of gold for an equivalent weight of gold coins. Folks liked the coins because they more than just represented real money, they were real money.

Sometimes solutions bring new problems. The gold coins in circulation started getting smaller. Gold is soft and it rubbed off on people's fingers, as it was slid over countertops, and in their pockets. And of course, there was always Peter. Every time Peter handled a gold coin, he made off with a little gold. Peter used his pen knife to shave off just the smallest sliver of gold from the circumference of each gold coin. After a while, his pile of gold shavings grew into a significant pile. Meanwhile, the gold coins kept getting smaller and smaller in diameter. Folks did not like the coins anymore because they could not be trusted to be real money. A one-eighth ounce gold coin no longer weighed one-eighth of an ounce.

Sheila and Susie decided to have a family Thanksgiving dinner at their Uncle's house. Besides understanding the value of families and traditions, they also knew their Uncle. Sam was very creative and was known as a problem solver. After the second piece of pumpkin pie, Sheila and Susie sat on the couch with their Uncle Sam and presented their problems. Uncle Sam told them he would have to get back to them but he had some ideas. He then fell fast asleep.

Here is what Uncle Sam came up with. "Sheila and Susie, we need to have some sort of standard. The certificates need to be interchangeable and the coins need to be trustworthy. The idea of only keeping a fraction of the real money deposits in the vaults might be good for the economy as long as folks understand what you are doing. I think they would accept the risks if they were compensated. You could call it a savings and loan. Some folks might put their real money in the vault both for safe keeping and for an investment. Of course, they would expect some sort of reasonable return if they knew there was a chance that they could lose their money. When you lend out their money, it helps other folks build and expand business. As long as everything is on the up and up, we all win. Transparency and mutual trust would be key elements in this system.

And about those coins…. If you mixed a harder metal in with the silver or gold, the coins would wear better. Once again, as long as everyone knows about it, everyone should accept it. An alloy of 90% silver and 10% copper should be about the right mix. But that should not be changed once it is in place. I even have an idea of how to take care of Peter's problem with his pen knife. When you make the coins, put some ridges on the outside rim. That way you could easily detect if someone was shaving off a little silver or gold. You know, our federal government is probably the best folks to make sure that business and commerce are kept fair. I tell you what. I have some verbiage we might put in a document that will protect us all. I will give it to Thomas, a buddy of mine, and see where he goes with it."

- "Congress shall have the power to coin Money, regulate the Value thereof, and of foreign Coin, and fix the Standard of Weights and Measures."
- "Congress shall have the power to provide for the Punishment of counterfeiting the Securities and current Coin of the United States."

- "No State shall make any Thing but gold and silver Coin a Tender in Payment of Debts."
- "No direct tax shall be laid unless in Proportion to the Census or Enumeration."

This means that everyone gets taxed at the same rate. I really like this last one.

It would be a good idea for the government to mint the coins and print the certificates. They can be trusted. We do not know if we will be able to trust the government long term though. To preserve the trust, we should ask them to print something like this on the currency."SILVER CERTIFICATE. This certifies that there is on deposit in the Treasury of The United States of America, One Dollar in silver, payable to the bearer on demand." I think that the term "dollar" should be used instead of ounces. Although the unit "dollar" comes from an old Bohemian silver coin, we can use it too. This will account for the alloy we are going to use to make the coins more durable. One silver certificate dollar is equal to the one real money silver dollar. As long as they can be exchanged freely back and forth, the dollar certificate will continue to represent real money.

Thanks to Thomas, Uncle Sam's plans were implemented. Sheila's and Susie's descendants as well as the people of the United States prospered. Unfortunately, Sandy also procreated. Remember Sandy?

Sandy had a son he called "Nathan Mayer," bless his heart. Nathan was a greedy little man. A banker by trade, he wanted to make even more money. He kept pressuring governments around the world to have a single unified, centralized banking system (with his siblings and descendants in charge, of course). One by one, governments all succumbed to the lure of being able to borrow at will with no accountability. There was only one holdout, the good old US of A. The only thing Nathan Mayer was able to convince our federal government to do was to establish a time-limited central bank charter that expired after a few years. And that was only to be able to finance wars. What a coincidence wars always cropped up and created a need to renew the U.S. central bank charter (Revolutionary War, War of 1812, Civil War, World War I). But what is a little war among friends? These central banks allowed for the creation of currency (not money) from out of thin air. The federal government loved it. There would be no limits on their ability to spend.

Sandy's descendants had even more grandiose ideas. What if they could disassociate real money from the currency? They could suck most of the real money right out of the real workers pockets through interest payments. It would be a continuous revenue stream. They would be perpetually good to go. Only one problem though. The revenue stream could not be sustained unless there was a permanent central bank and a way for the federal government to get their hands on the real money (income tax). Although the central bank would appear to be a governmental agency (Hey, let's call it The Federal Reserve Bank!), it would be a private bank with no auditing allowed and no one will ever know who really owns it. How about this for a project plan?

Date   Activity

- February 3, 1913   Implement income tax without regard to any census or enumeration.
- December 23, 1913 Establish permanent Federal Reserve Bank (FRB).
- 1914   Start issuing Federal Reserve Notes (FRN) – a "note" of IOU to the Federal Reserve Bank (FRB) with interest due.

- April 5, 1933   Pass Executive Order "forbidding the Hoarding of gold coin, gold bullion, and gold certificates within the United States".
- May 1, 1933   Last day for all U.S. citizens to turn in their gold to the Federal Reserve Bank in exchange for FRNs at $20.67 per ounce.
- 1933   Pass Emergency Banking Act and cease redemption of gold certificates for gold.
- 1934   Pass Gold Reserve Act and raise price of gold to $32 per ounce.
- March 1964   Halt redemption of silver certificates for coined silver dollars.
- 1965   Remove all silver from US coinage.
- June 24, 1968   Cease redeeming silver certificates for silver granules.
- August 15, 1971   Cease converting dollars to gold at a fixed rate.

Silver and Gold versus Dollar (FRN) Price Timeline (per ounce)

Year	Gold	Silver
1786	$19.49	$1.29
1933	$20.67	$0.44
1934	$32.00	$0.54
2012	$1,700.00	$30.77
2013	$1,354.30	$22.51

The above table holds the dollar constant and the price of gold fluctuates. It might be more interesting to hold an ounce of gold constant and see how the dollar fluctuated. That way you could see how well Nathan's plan worked.

Dollar (FRN) versus Gold and Silver Timeline (per ounce)

....or how many ounces you could buy with one

dollar

Year	Gold	Silver
• 1786	.0513	.7752
• 1933	.0484	2.2727
• 1934	.0313	1.8519
• 2012	.0006	.0325
• 2013	.0007	.04444

Another interesting table to look at is the value of your dated coins in today's FRNs.

	Nickel	Dime	Quarter	Dollar
• 1964	$0.045	$1.63	$4.07	$17.42
• 2013	$0.05	$0.10	$0.25	$1.00

And that my friend, is the end of the fable. Is it all really a fable?

FINANCES

Your Financial Future

A *Real Life Prepper* has to think about their financial future whether or not the schumer hits the fan. Although this may seem out of context, it is near and dear to RLP's heart and I highly recommend you think about it. The easiest and best way to start your financial preparation journey is to prepare a Simplified Income Plan (SIP) [A013] invented by RLP. I suggest that it will take you no more than 30 minutes to prepare but give valuable insight and a general direction to follow if you desire.

In essence, it is a simple breakdown of your monthly and annual income for the rest of your life. You probably know exactly how much money from what source you will make in January of 2013. You also know the same thing for October of 2015 (when you retire), for the month that you decide to start drawing social security, and what is going to be available for your family when they survive you (whenever that is).

If you can track projections, you can make plans to supplement, enhance, or mitigate risks. If you do not know what is going on, you cannot take any actions to make it better. What is the best option? Should you have $100,000 in the bank or should you have a "guaranteed" check come in at $5,000 every month for the rest of your life? In order to retire comfortably, you should expect to make about 70% to 80% of what you are living on comfortably while working. Do yourself and your family a favor and make your own plan. You will thank RLP later.

Here is an example of a SIP. This purposely does not factor in raises, COLA, taxes, expenses, or other assets like life insurance. Keep it simple.

Simplified Income Plan

Source	January 2013 (Today)	October 2015 (Retirement)	March 2017 (Start drawing SSA)	Upon Survival
Regular salary	$60,000	$12,000	$12,000	$6,000
SSA	$0	$0	$18,000	$9,000
Monthly	$5,000	$1,000	$2,500	$1,250
Annual	$60,000	$12,000	$30,000	$15,000

Can you both survive and thrive like this? Now you can start making plans to strengthen what you need to. For instance, should you look for advancement, a part-time job, or invest more in an IRA? What kind of life insurance do you need to provide for your survivors?

Cash

You may have heard the old adage that "cash is king." That may be truer than you realize. There are a variety of reasons you may want to have cash available. If you use a credit card to make a purchase, several things happen or have to happen.

Most of the time, you have to have electricity. I have seen some folks swiping credit cards on their iPhone attachment and of course, the iPhone still uses electricity in the form of a charge. The days of getting a physical imprint of a credit card using that little machine are probably long behind us. Although I have experienced vendors writing down the credit card number to charge later, most of them want to verify the card before they give you the goods. In most cases, this means they have to have a viable internet connection. If you take this a step further, you realize that ATMs and self-pay gas pumps will not work without electricity and the internet. You may not be able to purchase gasoline at all with a credit card if the internet is down.

The credit card companies maintain large databases. They know everything you ever bought (and when you bought it) with the card. It would not take very much for them to release that information to the government, marketers, or to have it stolen. Picture yourself going into a gun show. You are preparing to attend an Appleseed event. You need 1,000 rounds of .223. After shopping around for availability and price, you decide to buy from the big guy who brings his own wheeled leather chair to every show (you know who he is). The fact that you purchased 1,000 rounds of ammunition for the evil, black, assault rifle (read that with tongue-in-cheek) is now known to everyone who accesses the credit card database. Alternatively, you bring in a bunch of twenty dollar bills. This time, you peel off enough cash to walk away with the heavy box and you are totally anonymous. Which situation would you prefer?

Some vendors do not take credit cards at all. And virtually all vendors that do take credit cards have to pay a fee for every transaction. The fee may be between one and three percent. With cash, you may be able to negotiate a discount. Put yourself in the vendor's shoes for just a minute. You only have one basket of tomatoes left to sell. At exactly the same time, two folks offer to pay you the same price for your tomatoes. One has a credit card, the other has cash. Other than acting like Solomon, to whom do you sell the tomatoes?

Consider another scenario. You are on a road trip when the region loses internet connectivity. You are not paying attention until the low gas light on your dashboard actuates. When you pull over to the only gas station that is open within 25 miles, you see the hand written sign, "CASH ONLY." There are only so many pennies and nickels stuck in the seat cushions of your car.

Fortunately, I have a good friend with a prepper mindset. He encouraged me to stash some cash. We decided on mixed, smaller denominations because many folks do not even know who Grover Cleveland was nor do they trust $100 bills. It did not take as long as I thought it would to accumulate the suggested amount. The emergency cash stays in the envelope in the safe (you do have a safe, don't you?) and comes out when we go shopping where we want to maintain our privacy. From a psychological standpoint, it is also harder to make an impulse buy with cash than it is with a credit card. RLP recommends you have between $500 and $1,000 in your cash stash.

Financial Privacy

Some folks worry that every purchase you make over the internet or with a credit card is tracked by either our government or by untrustworthy businesses. RLP is not here to disagree with either theory. Clearly, cash (under a certain value) is the way to go to maintain maximum privacy, but it is hard to pay cash to Amazon over the internet for some wheat. Your credit cards are already being tracked and if an integrated picture of your purchases is developed, you may be considered as crazy as RLP. Not likely, but it could be close.

An alternative is to purchase gift cards (with a number on them) locally for cash. Use a variety of stores and locations. Then use the gift cards to purchase that wheat from Amazon. Direct your shipments to an address that makes sense to your privacy.

Silver and Gold

Some investment advisors recommend you purchase gold and silver as an investment. This may be a good and may be a bad idea. We will only address the *Real Life Prepper* aspect of silver and gold. It is still an investment, but an investment of a different kind. We recommend you start out with junk silver.

Junk Silver

Junk silver is not junk, that is just what it is called. Some folks collect old and rare coins. Their value is in their collectability. Those types of coins may or may not be good for your long term investment strategy. But they are not junk silver. Back in the day when our government actually knew what the Constitution said, we made our coins out of silver – actually they were 90% silver. This stopped in 1965. Those coins, called junk silver, are still in circulation. In all practicality, they are not really in circulation because many folks see their real value and replace them with fiat coins. If you see a dime, quarter, half-dollar, or dollar coin dated 1964 or earlier, grab it while you can. A great online resource for you is [L012] http://www.coinflation.com/ It is a play on words between coin and inflation. When this paragraph was written, a 1964 dime had a metal value of $1.45 in Federal Reserve Notes (FRN). A 1965 dime had a metal value of $0.017 or less than two cents. Whether you pay your taxes with the 1964 or 1965 dime, they will only credit you with $0.10 or ten cents.

You may think about investing in silver bars or ingots. Some of those are counterfeit, no longer weigh what they once did, are not easily recognized, or are not trusted. Everyone knows what a dime looks like.

Junk silver can be acquired from your local coin dealer, ebay, or online. One company that sells junk silver, including $1,000 face value bags is [L013]

http://www.monex.com/prods/silver_90.html. Another
site is [L014] http://www.gainesvillecoins.com/.
Generally, junk silver can be acquired at a smaller
premium than silver bars, rounds, or coins such as Silver
Eagles.

Gold

Silver is sometimes called the poor man's gold.
Gold is considerably more expensive than silver. It is
more value dense. Today, a one-ounce silver bar costs
$22.16 with a credit card ($21.52 with cash) and a one-
ounce gold bar costs $1,320.32 with a credit card
($1,281.99 with cash). Gold is more often counterfeited.
Silver is more easily recognized when in coin format
and more easily traded. I would not feel as bad trading a
one ounce silver bar for a loaf of bread than I would feel
if I traded a one ounce gold bar for the same loaf.

Inflation

Some folks believe that inflation is our greatest
threat. Urban legends abound about the hyper-inflation
in Germany after World War I. At the beginning of the
war, one U.S. dollar was worth 4.2 German Marks. In
1923, one U.S. dollar was worth 4,210,500,000,000
German marks. Germans battled the inflation by
purchasing hard goods in the morning rather than
waiting until the afternoon. One story relates how a
farmer paid off his farm mortgage with a single egg.

During a visit to Brazil during a period of high
inflation, I experienced an interesting phenomenon.
Although Brazil periodically exchanged their paper
currency (essentially just knocking off a zero), they
never changed their coins. You can look at it this way.
Four quarters equals one old dollar. Four quarters equals
one new dollar (which used to be ten dollars). Printing
currency is cheap. Minting coins is expensive.

Imagine if you had $1,000 extra to spare. You

want to both protect that $1,000 and help prepare your family for some sort of disaster. You could choose to put that $1,000 in the bank where you might get a 1% return. What would current inflation rates do to the value of your $1,000 in ten years? Another option is to buy a year's supply of long term storage food for your family ($1,000 for illustration purposes only). Barring a disaster, in ten years you will still have a year's supply of food. RLP does not recommend you go out and immediately invest all of your extra money into long term food storage. We recommend a thoughtful, balanced, and logical approach.

Nickels

I thank James Wesley Rawles for first bringing this to my attention. You pay a premium for junk silver coins. Although they will never lose their face value (a dime will always be worth a dime), the underlying metal price demands a premium and can fluctuate. Whereas silver is the poor man's gold, nickel may be the poor man's silver. There is no current premium for nickels. Although they may have to be ordered, you can go into any bank to buy nickels. $100 of nickels (in a box that weighs 22 pounds by the way) costs $100 with no premium. It makes a great gift for newborns. Coinflation [L049} http://www.coinflation.com/ lists the current metal value of a nickel at $0.043 or almost five cents. I have seen it at six cents when the price of nickel is up. The current metal value of a 1964 or a 2013 nickel is about 87% of its face value. The metal value of a 2013 dime is about 17% of its face value. The U.S. Mint is scheduled to change the metal content of nickels making them worth less. Remember what happened to dimes in 1965? If you get tired of the nickels, change them back into FRNs at no loss.

Bartering

Bartering is older than money. Unlike the

world's oldest profession, bartering is not illegal. (Hey NSA, nothing in this book is designed to promote any sort of tax evasion or breaking of laws.) Sorry for the commercial, back to bartering. So what is bartering, why would we barter, and with what do we barter? These are all good questions. Although Google is not your friend, you can learn a lot from the internet and even find entire websites specializing in bartering. There is a separate section of Craig's list just for bartering. So Google away – or better yet, DuckDuckGo or StartPage away.

Bartering is simply the trading of goods and services without the use of currency. Please read "Real Money: A Fable" if you need to understand a little about money and currency. I have a box of Malted Milk Balls. You have a Mounds bar. We trade – we have just bartered. So why would you want to, or have to, barter? Regardless of the reason, if there is no other way to transact business, we might have to barter. I want a gallon of gasoline and there is no way to give the gas station operator a credit card and she will not take cash. I agree to clean the bathrooms; she agrees to give me a gallon of gas. (For that, she should probably fill up my truck and my car!) The government may not like this arrangement because they cannot tax the transaction. Remember the government adage, "If it moves, tax it. If it does not move, regulate it." (Sorry NSA, just injecting a little humor. No offense intended.)

Let's take a brief look at what we can barter. You may want to acquire some barter goods as part of your preparations. Timing is a factor, too. Not too many people are going to line up today to trade with you for some toilet paper. In the future, who knows? I used to think a brick (around 500 rounds) of 22LR was expensive at $20. I have seen it lately at Gun Shows for $120 per brick – and there was only one brick available. If you think ammo is okay to trade (some folks do not),

22LR might fit the bill. It has intrinsic value. It retains its value, it is recognizable, and it is divisible. Here are some other ideas.

Bartering Products

- One ounce bottles of universal 2-cycle engine oil
- Feminine hygiene products
- Tobacco products
- Alcohol miniatures
- Batteries
- Ammunition
- Gasoline
- Propane (small bottles or recharge of small bottles)
- Fish hooks

Bartering Services

- Knife sharpening
- Battery recharging
- Wheat grinding
- Cleaning water
- Tilling land

ENERGY AND POWER

I love my electric blanket. I use it to take the chill off the sheets so that I can fall asleep fast. What a luxury! And before we go to bed, we watch one episode of *Arrow* or *The Dick Van Dyke Show* from years past on Netflix. In a time of need, we may not have those types of luxuries. Without taking some precautions and making some preparations, we may not even have the luxuries of ice cubes, frozen vegetables, cold milk, a warm house, or refrigerated insulin. And what would we do if we could not charge up our cell phones or radios? We need power and that means we need energy.

Energy normally comes to us, to our homes. And sometimes we have to go get it – think gasoline for your car or batteries from the store. You might be surprised at the impact of energy and power on your life's activities. A disruption in the supply of your energy and power will have major consequences. The first step in preparing for this type of event is performing an energy analysis. An Energy Analysis template [A007] is provided to help you get started. The purpose of the energy analysis is to have the *Real Life Prepper* do a little navel gazing.

Energy Analysis

Use the template provided to point you in the right direction. The objective is to determine what you use energy for and what alternatives you are prepared to deploy in case your normal supply gets disrupted. It is not sufficient to look at your energy life from a theoretical viewpoint only. You need to be prepared, practiced, and practical. RLP recommends you conduct a room by room survey. List all of the functions or tasks you perform in that room and/or all of the pieces of equipment you use in that room. The survey should lead to questions and they might lead to more questions. Ultimately this should lead you to some answers. Do not ignore any room.

For instance, visit your garage. Normally you operate your garage door using a remote or a push button. What would you do if there was no electricity? Does every member of your family (who has the requirement) know how to open, close, and secure the garage door with no electricity? Are they physically strong enough? Can they reach the controls? Are they practiced?

Let's dissect a single function in the kitchen and see how it can lead down multiple paths. We use a refrigerator to keep some of our food fresh. It runs on electricity. Providing electricity from your own generator is only one alternative. First let's look at the generator issue then explore some alternatives.

A generator can be portable or built-in. It should be of sufficient capacity to meet your needs. Running your refrigerator may be a need whereas running your electric blanket may only be a want. Choosing a generator solution is not a trivial exercise. What fuel will you use? How much fuel should you store? How do you keep the fuel safe and viable? Where will you locate the generator while operating? Does the noise or exhaust present a danger? Are there any governmental restrictions on fuel storage or generator operation? How will you get the power from the generator to the refrigerator? Will you use a transfer switch? Can all (who need to) successfully start and operate the generator? Do you need a backup to the generator? How often do you need to test the generator or practice your operations?

As with most things, there are alternatives to using a generator to supply electricity to your refrigerator. If it is a short-term outage, you may simply just not open your refrigerator door. You could have a neighborhood cookout and eat the food. You could preserve some of the food. You could buy some ice and put your food in coolers. You could simply break out the propane refrigerator you have in your basement and transfer the refrigerated food there. You may want to throw away some of the food before it spoils and drives you out of the kitchen.

The reason we recommend doing a thoughtful energy analysis is because how we use energy and power is more complex than we think it is at first glance. For instance, can we operate our natural gas range top if the electricity goes out? The answer is, "yes, no, maybe." The exhaust fan no longer works without electricity and if I am cooking, we need an exhaust fan. Each burner uses electrical power to generate a spark that initially ignites the gas. No electricity means I need matches.

Lighting is another example that requires thinking it through. Although our house is fairly new, the builder did not always make the best choices. The very nice kitchen has some natural lighting through windows but it can get very dark on the counters under the cabinets. The builder chose to mount heat-generating and fragile halogen lights under the cabinets. I wisely decided to replace them with very reliable and efficient LED lights. Following the builder's lead, I used the same hard wiring as the replaced halogen lights. There is no "regular" plug like a desk lamp since they are hard wired directly into a breaker. You cannot use an extension cord to power them. If I use an extension cord to power the refrigerator from the generator during an electrical outage, my under-cabinet LED lights stay dark.

Energy

All energy ultimately comes from fuel. Your own body heat and thinking efforts come from the burning of calories. Electricity comes from a generator that burns uranium, coal, natural gas, propane, diesel, gasoline, biomass, or something similar. Even hydro, wind, and solar generated electricity comes from the burning of the sun. Chances are that you are not going to have a miniature sun or nuclear reactor in your basement so we need to explore other fuels.

Fuel

Discounting the energy that is delivered to your home, for the *Real Life Prepper*, there are only a few viable fuel types that make sense. Practical fuel types share some common characteristics and a few requirements. Supplied ratings are relative and may change over time. On this subjective scale of 1 to 9, the higher number means better. Coal is relatively cheap and available but MrsRLP would not want to shovel coal into her stove every morning so she could fix breakfast.

Practical Fuel Characteristics

	Gasoline	Diesel	Kerosene	Propane	Wood
Expense	5	4	7	6	8
Availability	9	6	7	9	6
Handling Ease	4	5	6	5	8
Portability	6	8	8	8	5
Multiple Use	9	5	7	7	3
Safety	5	8	8	7	6
Longevity	5	7	8	9	7

Gasoline

I love gasoline as a fuel but that is probably because of the familiarity. I also hate gasoline. Gasoline is currently the most available and well known fuel. Unfortunately, for some nefarious purpose, we have folks who are willing to destroy the environment and the economy by forcing us to use gasoline made out of food. Most home generators, most cars, and most homeowner trucks run on gasoline. Most lawn mowers, most chain saws, most tillers, and many weed eaters run on gasoline.

Gasoline can be dangerous. Wanting to extend the range of my truck, I searched with no success for a cheap extra gasoline tank to be mounted in the bed. Note that extra diesel tanks are available at almost every corner store. If you decide to store extra gasoline, do not store it in your house. The liquid form of the gasoline is not really that dangerous. The fumes contain most of the risk. Imagine that you have an energy efficient natural gas hot water heater in your basement. Rather than using a constant-on pilot light, it uses a generated spark to ignite the natural gas when the water in the tank cools down. The gasoline cans you have stored in your garage leak. The fumes, being heavier than air, collect to a depth of one foot. Everything is okay until your teenage daughter takes a shower. The resultant explosion levels a city block. You were not properly prepared.

Gasoline Storage Containers

We recommend that you consider storing some gasoline if you have equipment that uses gasoline as a fuel. When the grid goes down and the local gas station pumps do not work, you can use the stored gasoline in your car or truck. I know you are surprised, but we have a system. How much you store depends on you and how much the regulators dictating your every move allow you to store.

Gasoline weighs about the same as water or eight (8) pounds per gallon. This means a five (5) gallon gasoline container will weigh about 40 pounds. I consider the five (5) gallon container the optimum size for storage and the two (2) gallon can the optimum size for the lawn mower.

Should you use a plastic container, which is cheaper and lighter and does not rust, or a metal container? Most cheap plastic containers breathe. This means that the plastic itself can be semi-permeable to gasoline, air, moisture, or light. Usually the cheaper, red cans you see everywhere suffer from these problems. If you have used this type of plastic container in the past, you have experienced the danger of sloshing and the "glug-glug" as air is allowed back into the container. Unfortunately, more enviro-terrorists force C.A.R.B. and nozzle rules on us that make these containers dangerous to us and the environment as well as hard to use. There are ways to fix these containers. Search eBay for "yellow vent caps." I call them "yella-thangs." Make sure you get the heavy duty kind with the retention lip.

Drill a hole in the new, dry, plastic container and add your own vent. You will find the containers are safer for you and friendlier to the environment. Instructions for making common sense modifications to the dangerous and hard-to-use nozzles are also available on YouTube.

Scepter makes some plastic military fuel cans (MFC) that are reported to be much better. The supplied nozzles still seem to be a problem.

The metal, NATO, gas cans and nozzles seem to be a very nice solution. RLP recommends [L025] http://www.jerrycan.com/ . Similar metal, NATO-like, gas cans are available on Amazon or elsewhere and may or may not be of the same quality construction. Use the information on jerrycan.com to make your comparisons. Make sure you know what you are getting.

Gasoline Storage System

When you store gasoline, you store it for a reason. You want it to be viable when you decide to use it. This means you have to apply the same rotation principles you use for your food. RLP has designed a system that balances effort and gasoline viability. It is easy to start out slow and build as you need to. Try to purchase the same type and size of containers. One cycle for your stored gasoline lasts 12 months or one year. If you elect to use five gallon containers, you will have 60 gallons of gasoline stored at any one time. Label each container with the month and a number. The first container will be labeled "January 1." Subsequent cans will be labeled, "February 1," "March 1," etc. If for some reason you decide to have two January cans, label the second January can, "January 2."

In January, take your year-old gasoline from your "January 1" can and pour it into your car or truck tank. Take your empty "January 1" container to the gas station (hopefully a pure gas station) and refill it. Treat the new gasoline at double the normal dose, seal it well, shake, and safely store it until the next January. Your gasoline will remain viable for at least a year if stored properly. Repeat this action once a month for the gasoline container with the same label. If you skip a month, use it up the next month. If you cannot afford or do not want to purchase and store 12 containers, there is nothing wrong with choosing any number of months you want. However, the gasoline vendors make better gasoline in the winter months than in the summer months. I know people who only have a "January 1" and a "February 1" container.

Gasoline Transfer

This is why I hate gasoline. Some idiot decided to put the fill hole in your gas tank of your car on the side of the car. It should be on the top so I can fill it up like they do in a NASCAR pit. Gravity is your friend. It is extremely difficult to hold up a 40 pound gas can and pour gasoline into that very restrictive opening while simultaneously trying to operate the funky nozzle designed by an enviro-terrorist. You might even think they do not want you to do that.

Gasoline is dangerous. Please do not try to use an electric pump or spark generating system to transfer gasoline. Use only an approved, UL listed pump. Or take your chances.

The simplest gasoline transfer device (other than pouring through a nozzle or funnel) is the siphon. You might regret trying to siphon gasoline out of a tank with your mouth. However, for between $6 and $15, you can purchase a self-priming, copper jiggler pump. This is essentially a plastic see-through hose with a copper ball check valve on one end. You "jiggle" the valve in the fluid to start the siphon and gravity takes over. Another siphon choice has a squeeze ball to initiate the fluid transfer. Note that both of these eventually rely on gravity. If your receiving tank is higher than your supply tank, you will run into problems.

For around $7-$15, you can get a plunger/piston type Multi-Use Transfer pump from Harbor Freight or Amazon. These have an advantage in that as long as you have not contaminated them, you can use them for other purposes such as transferring oil or pumping air. Think of these pumps as disposable.

The next type of device also uses a manual pump. One such manual pump is called the Jack Rabbit pump at around $50. Try the Black and Decker or Ace Hardware brand. This is a rotary pump which you have to continually crank. These have an advantage in that they use a separate intake and discharge hose and you can pump uphill.

At the next level, you have the gas caddy. DuraMax makes a $100-$140, 14-gallon gas can on wheels (Flo n' Go). For those of you keeping track, it weighs almost 120 pounds when full. It comes with a MaxFlo Siphon Pump that you squeeze to get started. You can continue to squeeze to pump uphill but the best thing to do is to use the squeeze just to get the siphon started. I found that it is easier to manhandle the Flo n' Go onto the top of my truck tool box and then let gravity drain the 14 gallons into the truck tank. This is particularly useful when you are transferring more than 14 gallons. Use the Flo n' Go system but pour the five gallon cans into the Flo n' Go. The MaxFlo Siphon pump is also sold separately.

A nicer gas caddy is the Roughneck 30-gallon fuel caddy. At $450-$520 and 350 pounds when full, it better be nice. It comes with a metal, two-way, rotary transfer pump that requires 12 revolutions per gallon. I want one for Christmas. The rotary transfer pump (and even an UL approved electric version) is also available separately.

The top end is to just buy an electric gas pump like you see at the gas station. Besides being big, ugly, and expensive, they also need electricity to operate.

Ethanol in Gasoline and Treating

The primary enemy of both gasoline and diesel is moisture. There is moisture in the air and the moisture is easily transferred to the fuel. Alcohol actually attracts moisture and pulls it out of the air. The best thing you can do to preserve the viability of your fuel is to keep the tanks full. The second best thing you can do is to keep the tanks at a reasonable, constant temperature. Underground storage tanks do a lot better than aboveground tanks. This applies to both storage tanks and equipment tanks. For instance, when you store a lawn mower at the end of the season, either completely drain the tank and run the engine fuel-dry, or completely fill up the tank (with treated gas) so there is no air whatsoever in the tank.

Although there are various reports on ethanol and non-ethanol (pure gas) benefits and hazards, we can all agree that there are issues. If you believe that pure gas lasts longer or gets better gas mileage, you may want to know where you can purchase it. Regardless, RLP recommends you only use pure gas for storage. Did you know that all gasoline in Alaska is ethanol free? There has to be some reasoning for that. One way to find a pure gas station is to search the internet. One helpful site is [L026] http://pure-gas.org/ . They have a list of stations by state (with some printing options) and links to both the iPhone App Store and the Android Google play store for your smart phone.

Another useful site is [L027] www.buyrealgas.com. Note that pure-gas.org and buyrealgas.com do not necessarily agree on the gas stations. Buyrealgas.com has an interesting link to [L028] www.fueltestkit.com where you can buy an alcohol and water test kit for about $30. The fueltestkit.com website has some compelling information about the risk of ethanol additives in gasoline. I highly recommend you consult the table they publish regarding "Is your gas additive safe with E10 fuel?" They make recommendations about the safety of various additives including Sta-bil, PRI-G, and Seafoam. Many of these additives include alcohol. The fueltestkit.com website suggests that GAS-SHOK might be the best additive if you are going to use one. GAS-SHOK is available from the [L029] http://usafuelservice.com/ website and some retailers. One ounce treats ten gallons and the smallest (8-oz) bottle sells for about $18.

Sta-Bil

Sta-Bil comes in colors! The red Sta-Bil is the older stuff, used before ethanol was mixed with real gasoline. It was used to stabilize the gasoline for storage up to one year. The blue Sta-Bil is the marine formula. Blue Sta-Bil is used to protect against the damaging effects of ethanol blended fuels since the ethanol (alcohol) attracts water and marine engines are near water. Do yourself a favor. Use only blue, Marine Stab-Bil and do not worry about it. Both the red and the blue Sta-Bil can be used by measuring directly from the squeeze bottle.

Measuring PRI-G

RLP has been a loyal Sta-Bil user for many years. Always trying to find something better, I recently purchased a pint (16 fl oz) of PRI-G "Super Concentrated" to try out. The pint of PRI-G treats 256 gallons of gasoline. The instructions say to add 1 fluid ounce to 16 gallons of gasoline. The squeeze bottle is marked out with a 1/2 ounce mark and 1 ounce mark. That does not help me treat my two-gallon cans, my five-gallon cans, or my 14-gallon cans.

Time to break out the U.S. conversion tables.

- One (1) fluid ounce is six (6) teaspoons

- One (1) fluid ounce is 29.57 (roughly 30) milliliters

- One (1) fluid ounce is ~591 drops

So, I can take one of MrsRLP's measuring spoons and treat my gas. She will never know. It takes .0625 ounces, .375 tsp or 1.875 ml to treat one gallon of gas. Rounding up to "over treat," I made the following table. I am not going to count drops.

PRI-G Treatment Table

Gallons	Teaspoons (tsp)	ml
1	.5	2
2	1	4
5	2	10
14	5.5 or 6	27

I rotate the containers so that no can is really free for more than one day. I posted my "PRI-G Treatment Schedule" near the gas containers. Rather than using measuring spoons, I use calibrated syringes. A box of 100 10cc syringes (hypodermics without the needles) is about $17 from Amazon. P.S. One cc is one ml.

Diesel

I have yet to find a reasonable, sane, person who could explain to me technically why diesel fuel should cost more than gasoline. The only reason I could come up with is that it is a political move to try and move us away from diesel. I want a tractor. I want a diesel tractor. And I want the diesel to cost less than gasoline as it should. I could easily refuel my tractor, my pickup truck, and my generator with my own diesel storage tank.

Diesel engines generally last longer than gasoline engines. They produce more of their power at low RPMs while gasoline engines produce most of their power at high RPMS. Diesel fuel is generally more energy dense than gasoline. Diesel has about 147,000 BTUs per gallon while gasoline has about 125,000 BTUs per gallon. It should require less diesel fuel than gasoline to do the same amount of work. Diesel is safer. It is hard to ignite unless you want to ignite it. And diesel is cheaper to make.

Diesel works better than gasoline in tractors. Gasoline works better than diesel in race cars. In order to affect public policy, the federal government mandates that diesel come in certain colors. #2 heating fuel, otherwise known as diesel, must be dyed red. Off-road diesel (for farmer's tractors and such) must be dyed blue-green. Regular on-road diesel (for truckers and such) must be colorless. This is to make sure the right taxes are collected. Whoa be to the trucker who gets caught with red diesel in his tanks.

Just as gasoline needs some preservative to maintain its viability in longer term storage, so does diesel. Diesel actually suffers more from possible biological contaminants. Diesel might need to be treated with a biocide and potentially a fungicide. You can use PRI-G to treat gasoline and PRI-D to treat diesel. You can reasonably expect diesel fuel to be viable for at least a year if stored properly. Treated, it should last longer. In general, diesel fuel will remain viable longer than gasoline.

Kerosene

Naphtha, gasoline, kerosene, and diesel all come from petroleum. The difference is where they are in the distillation process. Kerosene used to be called coal oil. Gasoline used to be called petroleum naphtha and was sold as a cleaning solvent before it was used as a fuel. More carbon atoms in the hydrocarbon molecules mean a higher boiling point. Naphtha with few carbon atoms (used in things like dry cleaning solvent) boils off first. Next comes gasoline, then kerosene, then diesel. Next comes lubricating oils, then tar, and finally asphalt which we use to make roads. Congratulations, you have just earned a Masters Degree in Petroleum Engineering.

All of that was just to tell you kerosene is almost like diesel. It just burns easier and cleaner. Diesel is named after the German engineer who invented the diesel engine in the late 1800s. Kerosene is derived from the Greek word for wax and was trademarked for years as a lamp oil.

For the *Real Life Prepper*, kerosene is primarily used for space heating and lighting. It can be used as engine fuel, but we will not go there. Do not try that at home. Normally you use the kerosene heat and light inside your house. It makes most sense to use only K-1 (low sulfur content) kerosene. It is the best and cleanest type. Kerosene should be clear with no particulates. Avoid yellow snow and yellow kerosene.

Kerosene could potentially have the same bacterial growth problems as diesel. However, kerosene is usually stored in a more stable environment than diesel and thus will probably be more stable. The effective storage life of kerosene can be 10 years or more.

Propane (LPG) versus Natural Gas

Propane is also a hydrocarbon and is a byproduct of natural gas production and petroleum refining. That means it is made only because of producing natural gas, or making gasoline, kerosene, and diesel. Propane is not pure. It is also known as Liquefied Petroleum Gas (LPG) or LP Gas. Propane is liquid at room temperature and is what you use in your outdoor grill.

Propane is not the same as natural gas or Compressed Natural Gas (CNG). Natural gas is what is piped into your home. Propane is normally purchased in 20 pound cylinders or tanks. These tanks are normally used for regular backyard grills. Natural gas is not liquid at room temperature. However, natural gas is sometimes shipped as Liquid Natural Gas (LNG).

You can use propane fuel for cars, forklifts, lawn mowers, weed eaters, and leaf blowers. Propane burns significantly cleaner than gasoline or diesel. Interestingly, it can be used as a paintball propellant (pressure only) and household air freshener sprays. Absorption refrigerators run off of the propane combustion with no electricity needed.

Propane is heavier than air so presents a risk if there is a leak where you could have a spark or open flame such as a hot water heater. The storage life of propane is virtually indefinite. Natural gas is lighter than air and thus may be safer in certain circumstances.

Generators

So how can you take all of that chemical energy stored in the petroleum products and turn it into electrical energy that you can use to cool your food in your regular refrigerator? The answer is a generator. A generator is what your utility company uses to make the electricity they send down the wires to your house. You pay a base charge for the connection to your house and then an extra charge for how much energy and power you use. In most states, if you send the electric company power back over the same wires, they have to pay you instead. Under normal conditions, it is not economical to run your generator to make electricity for the power company. But you could.

Think about it. The electricity can run in both directions. A storm takes out a big transformer that supplies your subdivision. Having read *Real Life Prepper*, you own a generator. You cautiously move it outside so the exhaust fumes do not poison your family. While you are getting your gasoline out of your long term storage, the utility company lineman is raising his bucket to work on the transformer. Just about the same time you get your generator started and plugged into the outlet, the lineman reaches in to reconnect the wires leading to your house. The shock is enough to blow the lineman right out of his bucket and on to the top of his bucket truck. You now have an opportunity to exercise some of the medical skills you learned.

This cautionary story is meant to teach you that electricity can be dangerous, even outside of your own home. Either learn how to do things safely and correctly or let a qualified electrician take care of you. Some folks will be tempted to make a male-to-male plug that connects your generator directly to your house. This is very dangerous and can lead to tragic consequences. The optimum solution is to use an automatic transfer switch. A more budget-conscious choice is to use a manual transfer switch. But, please use one or the other. The transfer switch makes sure that you cannot inappropriately back feed electricity into the lines outside of your house. Now that RLP has scared you, back to generators.

The big question in the world of generators is how big you want it to be. Harbor Freight sells a two-cycle, 800 watt generator for $130-$180. This is portable, loud, and big enough to power a small refrigerator or television set. Look for it on sale or use a coupon if you can and it is a great deal. Northern Tool sells a towable, Pramac, 175kW Diesel generator for only $50,000. The Pramac has a 260 gallon diesel fuel tank. It does not go on sale very often.

So how big a generator do you need? To answer that question, you need to understand watts. Simply put, one watt is one ampere (amp) times one volt. Normally you want 120 volts (some people call it 110 or 115 volts) delivered to your regular household outlet. A regular 60 watt light bulb draws ½ amp at 120 volts. Make yourself a table of the things you want to power from your generator. There is a sample [A008] Generator Sizing Table for you to use on the *Real Life Prepper* website. Use either the typical power rating (watts) or the nameplate data from the appliance. Multiply the amp rating times the voltage rating to give you the power rating.

Generator Sizing Table

Device	Typical Running Watts	Typical Starting Watts	Voltage	Amps	Typical Calculated Watts
Laser Printer	720	1440	120	5.4	648
Refrigerator	800	2400	120	5	600
Fan	200	600	120	3	600
Lamp	60	60	120	.5	60
Total	1800	4500	NA	13.9	1900

Note that there are two "typical" columns. Some electrical loads require more power to start than they require to just run. A typical electrical motor draws three times as much current to get started. A laser printer kicks on the fuser (a heavy duty heating element) when it starts up. When you size a generator, it must handle both starting load and running load. Name plate data may or may not give the starting load although they almost always give the running load. A typical generator rating will say something like this: 5500/6875. This means the generator is rated to handle a starting load of 6,875 watts and a running load of 5,500 watts.

Power Management

Sizing your generator for the zombie apocalypse is expensive, a waste of resources, and hard to do. An alternative is to manage your power plan. There are steps you can take to reduce your overall power needs and reduce the need for a generator with a large starting capacity. A typical incandescent bulb in your house uses 60 watts. An equivalent LED bulb uses 11 watts to provide the same amount of light. With LED bulbs, the *Real Life Prepper* is saving money through a reduced heat load and reduced power requirements on a day-to-day basis. A typical light bulb (incandescent or LED) requires the same amount of power to start or to run. A microwave oven typically uses the same amount of power to start or run. A garage door opener typically uses 1420 watts to start but only 720 watts to run. Think about how often you are going to use your garage door opener and how long it actually runs while operating.

You may want to consider not running all of your power consuming devices at the same time. If you keep your refrigerator and freezer doors closed, there is no reason to supply electricity to both of them at the same time. Power one, get it cool, and then power the other.

You definitely do not want to start every

appliance in the house at the same time. Start them in sequence and let the generator settle down to handle the load before you start the next appliance. Watch the movie *Apollo 13* again for inspiration.

RLP has difficulty suppressing his inner engineer. A more advanced *Real Life Prepper* may also want to take some real life measurements before deciding on a generator or coming up with some sort of power management plan. RLP recommends the purchase of a power measuring device such as the "Kill A Watt" manufactured by P3 International [L145} http://www.p3international.com/. Different models are available from Amazon and many big box stores. Besides, it will help you become the envy of your neighborhood buddies.

Generator Voltage and Power

Note also that all of the electrical devices in this table run at 120 volts. Many devices run at 240 volts such as a hot water heater, clothes dryer, or an oven. You can probably guess that 240 volt devices are more efficient. But you have to make sure your generator can supply the voltage you need. The *Doomsday Prepper* is even considering single phase and three-phase power. The *Real Life Prepper* normally uses only single-phase power and just wants to keep the food from spoiling. Small, consumer, gasoline generators are widely available and are a very good place to start. Wait for a good sale and pick up a cheap one to get started. Harbor Freight, Lowes, Costco, and Sam's already have enough choices to allow you to take care of some needs (such as a power backup for your refrigerator) and allow you to experiment at low cost.

RLP guesses that the typical household needs more than just a laser printer, refrigerator, fan, and a single lamp. You should use the Generator Sizing Table to size your own generator. You may end up with a whole house generator with an automatic transfer switch. In essence, it monitors the power coming from the street (your utility company). When the street power fails, the automatic transfer switch disconnects your house from the grid, starts the generator, and powers selected loads in your house. If you size the whole house generator large enough, everything will act normally until you run out of fuel or until the grid power comes back on. Then the automatic transfer switch will dump the generator (and all of the power in your house), reconnect to the grid, and restore grid power to your house. The whole house generators all start with batteries, just like your car.

RLP also guesses that most folks will not be able to or will not want to have a whole house generator. Smaller generators, properly outfitted, can be started by a switch and battery, or can be started by a pull cord similar to your lawn mower. The generator must be positioned so that the exhaust fumes are outside, not in your garage. It can, and will kill you.

You still need to get the power from the generator to your refrigerator! Pay close attention to the power outlets on the generator. Imagine that you have a 6,000 watt rated generator with one regular, household type, 120 volt electrical outlet. A regular household outlet has two plug sockets and normally the circuit supplying that duplex outlet can carry 15 amps. So if you treat it the same way as in your house, you can get (120 volts x 15 amps = 1800 watts) out of your generator. If you count each socket at 1800 watts, you can still only get 3,600 watts out of your 6,000 watt generator. Many generators have multiple outlets, 120 volt and 240 volt outlets, and/or Recreational Vehicle (RV) type outlets.

This is a picture of a typical home generator with two "normal" outlets plus a center NEMA L5-30 RV outlet. In order to effectively use those 30 amps, you must have a twist lock plug that fits.

Your generator is safely positioned so that the exhaust fumes are not going into your house. It is making noise that your neighbors can hear and smoke that you neighbors can smell. Everything else is quiet. Your refrigerator food is getting warmer. Although the generator is making electricity, none is getting into your house. Having seen *Doomsday Preppers*, you decide to make an extension cord with a male-to-male plug. You plug one male end into the generator outlet and grab the other male end to plug it into the household outlet next to your garage door. If you succeed in not shocking yourself, you successfully get electricity into your house for all of the circuits to use. Without a transfer switch, that electricity is also being supplied to the power pole outside and your neighbor's house. This is not smart. Life is hard. Life is harder if you are stupid. RLP does not recommend you making or using a male-to-male extension cord.

If you do not have an automatic transfer switch,

you can install a manual transfer switch. Alternatively, you can open up the main breaker supplying your house. Opening, or tripping, the main breaker will disconnect you from the grid. It does not disconnect the non-essential loads in your house from the limited power in the generator. One alternative is to install a separate breaker box for the essential loads in the house. Power your essential loads from the essential loads breaker box. When needed, disconnect the essential load breaker box from your main breaker box and power it separately from the generator.

A cheaper solution is to acquire a generator distribution box. The generator distribution box resides in your house with a long, weatherproof power cord. The power cord runs outside to your generator and plugs into the RV outlet at perhaps 30 amps or more. You then use regular extension cords that plug into the generator distribution box and run those cords to your individual essential loads. Making one penetration into your house for the generator distribution box is a lot easier than having multiple, long extension cords running from your outside generator, inside the house, up the stairs, around the corners, through the doors you can no longer close, to your essential loads. Some folks decide to have the appropriate, permanent, weatherproof power receptacle on the outside wall of the house for the generator connection.

Here is a picture of a homemade distribution box that takes advantage of the 30 amp RV outlet on the generator and powers multiple "typical" household type outlets.

Think about the implications of actually using your generator. Can you move it? Can you start it? How do you have the weatherproof power cord for the generator distribution box penetrate the weather and security barrier of your house? Do you have enough, and long enough, extension cords to power your essential loads? Do you even know what your essential loads are? Do you have written instructions and a checklist? Do you need to run your generator all of the time? How are you going to refuel the generator? How are you going to power your 240 volt hot water heater from your 120 volt generator? Can you even plug in an extension cord into your hot water heater, stove, clothes dryer, or air conditioner?

A typical, household, portable generator runs on gasoline. When you run out of gasoline, everything goes dark. A good resource for generator information is [L043] http://www.generatorjoe.net/store.asp where Joe talks about gasoline, diesel, propane, and natural gas powered generators. Joe even sells generators that are tri-fuel and run on gasoline, natural gas, or propane. Joe recommends a diesel generator for a lot of reasons. Joe's website may be the best source of unbiased generator information on the internet.

The typical, big-box store generator does not make very clean power. As the load on the generator changes, so does the speed of the engine. Since this is directly related to the quality of the power, it may not be the best for devices such as televisions or computers that rely on clean power. And it is noisy. An alternative to the typical generator like this is an inverter generator that makes clean power, is quieter, and is more efficient. They are typically made by Honda or Yamaha although there are a few other inverter generator brands. Inverter generators are typically more expensive.

Nobody said this was going to be easy. If it was easy, anybody could do it. Remember our essential rules. Try things out and practice them. Do more than just think about scenarios. Actually hook things up and make sure they work. Your refrigerator does not have to run all of the time. Perhaps you can run your refrigerator for a while then swap over to run your freezer for a while. Those extra frozen water bottles in your freezer will help to maintain the correct temperatures.

Extension cords

Do not try to get away with the cheap extension cords. Bright green or orange outdoor extension cords can work inside your house too. Some of those extension cords have plugs and outlets (ends) that light up when they are powered. Some have multiple outlets so you can run one long cord and then several shorter cords where needed.

The more amps you are drawing through the

extension cord, the thicker the wire (or heavier the gauge) the extension cord needs to be. Note that a heavier gauge cord is actually a smaller number. A 10 gauge extension cord can safely carry more current than a 16 gauge extension cord. A 10 gauge extension cord is considerably more expensive than a 16 gauge cord. Voltage drops as the cord gets longer. In order to minimize the voltage drop, you need to use a heavier gauge extension cord. For instance, a 25 foot, 14 gauge extension cord can safely carry 15 amps. If you need to extend that to 100 feet, you must use a 12 gauge extension cord. It may be handy to have your extension cords stored in the same place and labeled.

Solar Power

Solar will be mentioned briefly only for completeness. It deserves a lot more treatment and its own book. With the proper design, you can power a battery bank from the sun. While everything is normal, you can use your own generated electricity and sell the excess back to the power company. When the grid goes down, you can sustain your own loads for a while from your personal battery bank. Power generated in solar cells is direct current (DC) and you must use an inverter to make your alternating current (AC) that most of your electrical appliances use. Some prepper houses operate on DC only or on AC/DC appliances.

A typical solar (or wind) power system relies heavily on batteries that are similar to automobile, marine, or golf cart batteries. They can be expensive, are heavy, have to be maintained, and must be vented properly. RLP guesses that you are not a solar power battery expert but you have used flashlight batteries.

Energy Training

We all understand how critical energy is to our civilization. RLP recently found a fairly inexpensive (read that as free) way to increase your knowledge about energy. Start out with the course "Fundamentals of Power" and work your way through batteries and generators. There are more than 200 web based courses here.

Here is a friendly link that will take you to the Schneider Electric (APC) site.

[L030] http://www.myenergyuniversity.com

If you register, you can find out information about power, energy, racks, efficiency, etc. courses. There is also information regarding an industry certification called Professional Energy Manager (PEM). If you are involved in electricity in any way (pretend you still have electricity in your house), it might be to your advantage to at least take a few courses.

You will need Adobe Flash player and Adobe Shockwave installed to do the courses. You may have to use Google Chrome as your browser if you have other browser restrictions.

COMMUNICATIONS

Be aware that this can be a confusing and technical topic. RLP recommends you refer to the glossary for terms you may not be familiar with. You do not have to know everything here. Pick and choose what you are interested in and use some of the links for more education. RLP did not become this smart by just reading one chapter. Did I say that out loud?

Radio Communications

In a survival situation, radio communications boil down to two categories: listening and talking. You may want to do both. You can further refine those two categories depending on who you want to listen to and who you want to talk to.

Back in the day when I first started hunting, I purchased a Motorola TalkAbout Distance DPS radio (like a walkie-talkie). The walkie-talkie is more formally known as a handheld transceiver. I was not planning on just listening. I wanted to talk to my hunting buddies. So I got the same type of radio they had. It was expensive. The TalkAbout used both a rechargeable Ni-Cad battery pack and disposable AA alkaline batteries. Ten channels were on the dial: 1 through 7 then A, B, C, and S. Stay tuned to see why they add up to 11. I was told to put my radio dial on "C" because that was what they were using. Of course, I complied. I could not talk with them if we were not on the same frequency. Other than being expensive, this seemed very innocuous and benign.

My first real mistake was not completing my research before I bought the TalkAbout. When it arrived, I made my first recognizable mistake by partially reading the manual. A small section said that the TalkAbout operated on General Mobile Radio Service (GMRS) frequencies and required a FCC license. I was somewhat familiar (I thought) with the FCC license because I had to get one to operate a radio in a private plane. Accordingly, I went to the FCC website, registered, and signed up for the free license. Unfortunately, the FCC website was as bad then as the Affordable Care Act website was in 2013. It took almost ten years for the FCC to catch up to me with a bill for the $50 license fee and $100 fine for not paying for and renewing the license. Life is hard. Life is harder when you are stupid. My hunting buddies had not read the manual, had not registered with the FCC, and did not get any bills. Ignorance is bliss.

After using the TalkAbout for a few years, the Ni-Cad pack would not hold a charge. It took another couple of years before my replacement Ni-Cad pack also failed. Unwilling to make another $500 purchase for another TalkAbout, I started wondering if I could buy and use some of those cheap bubble-pack radios sold at every Walmart and Academy Sports across the country. It was time to dig the TalkAbout manual out of the unused hunting gear box and read the whole thing.

The first thing I discovered was that our chosen channel, C, was an emergency channel. Here I quote from the manual. "The emergency channel (C) is to be used only for the purpose of soliciting or rendering assistance to a traveller, or for communicating in an emergency pertaining to the immediate safety of life or the immediate protection of property. The emergency channel is used by certain organizations during emergency situations and is not necessarily monitored." No wonder we had no interference from other hunting clubs in the area! My hunting buddies were not happy when I asked them to change to channel 7 and we subsequently heard a lot of chatter from adjacent hunting clubs. It took some considerable effort to convince them to start using the interference eliminator codes. I then talked to them about bandwidth. The FCC requires that radios using the Family Radio Service (FRS) frequencies use a bandwidth of 12.5 kHz. The TalkAbouts come pre-set to a bandwidth of 25 kHz. One of my hunting buddies' head exploded. Another one fainted.

I did buy a bubble-pack of two Midland "Up to 36 Mile Two Way Radio" walkie-talkies. I set the channel to 7 on my Midland but could not talk to the TalkAbouts. I drove down the road 36 miles and could not talk to my wife on the companion Midland. My wife's eyes rolled up into the back of her head and she fainted. My head exploded.

Wouldn't it be nice if someone broke down all of that stuff so that we could use it in real life? We should not have to be experts on everything just to use it. What we need is to be able to talk to each other. Each family or group should use common equipment or at least common and compatible frequencies and codes (planned in advance) so they can communicate in an emergency. It may be the ubiquitous cheap walkie-talkies, it may be ham radios, it may be cell phones, and it may be semaphore. But it should work and it should be planned, tested, and effective.

Walkie-talkie Channels, Frequencies, and Codes

The common walkie-talkies we normally use operate in the ultra-high frequency (UHF) range. This is important because UHF is primarily a line of sight communication frequency. If you have a cordless phone, it operates on UHF. Regardless of what the package says, these radios have a tough time communicating at a range of 36 miles. Keep these three thumb rules in mind. 1. In general terms, the greater the advertised range for the same manufacturer, the better it will be. 2. Do not believe the manufacturer's advertised range. 3. Probably the best you are going to do is about five miles on a good day.

There are three types of these common walkie-talkies, FRS, GMRS, and FRS/GMRS. You are not required to get a FCC license for FRS-only communications. FRS is shorter range than GMRS. You do not need any license to purchase any of these radios, only to operate some of them but in only certain configurations. You do need a license to operate (transmit) on the GMRS frequencies and some of the shared frequencies. Just like the FM radio in your car sounds better than the AM radio, these FRS or GMRS radios (using FM) sound clearer than similar radios using AM. There are normally 22 channels used for FRS and GMRS walkie-talkies. They do not necessarily correspond between manufacturers. See the [A005] Walkie-Talkie Frequency Chart on the *Real Life Prepper* companion website for an example of how you can compare channels and frequencies.

Family Radio Service (FRS)

FRS has only been around in the United States since about 1996. Do not waste your time buying a FRS-only radio. FRS is limited to a power output of 500 milliwatts. That is a fancy way of saying one-half-of-one watt. Take a look at the walkie-talkie frequency table to see what channels FRS uses. Note that FRS and GMRS share channels 1 through 7. The only difference is the power output. You do not need a FCC license to broadcast at 462.5625 MHz (channel 1) when using one-half of a watt (FRS). You do need a FCC license to broadcast on that same frequency when using five watts (GMRS). You limit yourself, your range, and your communication flexibility when using FRS. Channels 8 through 14 are restricted to FRS only. The real life range of a FRS radio is about one mile.

General Mobile Radio Service (GMRS)

GMRS radios normally operate between one and five watts. The real life range of a GMRS walkie-talkie is about five miles. As previously mentioned, they share channels 1 through 7 with FRS. That means you can talk to a FRS radio at a greater range then they can talk to you. GMRS radios are not allowed to use channels 8 through 14. Channels 15 through 22 are restricted to GMRS radios only. You need a GMRS license to broadcast on any channel using GMRS.

In real life where you have a mix of FRS and GMRS radios, what channel would you choose to communicate within a particular group? The answer is channel 1 through 7 since both FRS and GMRS radios will operate in the FRS mode on these channels.

Although GMRS-only radios are available on the market, most of the consumer walkie-talkies are combination FRS/GMRS radios. That means they can operate on all 22 channels. They are in FRS mode when on channels 8 through 14 and GMRS mode when on the other channels.

Some commercial entities use GMRS-only walkie-talkies and base stations. GMRS repeaters are also available. Most 22-channel, bubble pack FRS/GMRS radios cannot use the repeaters.

Interference and Privacy Codes

Why can't we all get along? That is what the FCC wants to know. They expect all FRS and GMRS operators to politely share the allocated frequencies. There is nothing to prevent another family in your neighborhood from hogging all of the airtime on the channel you have selected for your group. You will be able to hear everything they say and they will be able to hear everything you say on the same channel. There is no privacy using FRS or GMRS radios.

Some manufacturers advertise that their radios have interference or privacy codes. These are primarily marketing terms. The terms are virtually synonymous. Sometimes they are called sub-channels. They are not sub-channels nor are they private. The interference codes essentially mute all of the radio transmissions that are not using the same interference code. That does not mean those transmissions are blocked. They simply appear muted to someone not using that interference code. The frequency/channel is still occupied when being used with a privacy code. This still causes interference when two radios are broadcasting on the same channel and different privacy codes at the same time. Even when you listen in on a channel before broadcasting and it is quiet, it may be in use by someone using a different privacy code. When you talk, you will talk over them.

Although there are others, there are only two primary interference or privacy code systems. Both Motorola and Midland can use the Continuous Tone-Coded Squelch System (CTCSS) and Digital Coded Squelch (DCS).

Here is a real life application. The Hatfields and the McCoys cleaned the local Walmart out of all their bubble-pack Midland walkie-talkies. After finding someone who could read, they studied the Communications chapter of *Real Life Prepper*. The Hatfields chose channel 16. After discovering that piece of intelligence, the McCoys also decided to use channel 16. All Hatfield communications were heard by the McCoys and all McCoy communications were heard by the Hatfields. Junior Hatfield convinced his family to configure their radios to use a privacy channel. They chose CTCSS code 37. The Hatfields no longer heard the McCoys and the McCoys no longer heard the Hatfields. Perfect – the feud was over. That is until both

the Hatfields and the McCoys decided they wanted to
have simultaneous conversations on channel 16. No one
had very much success hearing anyone else, even
members of their own family. The McCoys gave up and
shut up. Mildred McCoy got so frustrated that she just
started pushing buttons. Stumbling upon CTCSS privacy
code 37, she discovered that she could hear everything
the Hatfields were planning, including the details of
Junior's upcoming marriage proposal to Mildred.
Mildred convinced her family to switch to channel 17.
The Hatfields could talk without interference and the
McCoys could talk without interference. This time the
feud was really over. Feel free to update Wikipedia with
this information about the Hatfield-McCoy feud and cite
Real Life Prepper as the source.

FCC Licensing

No license is required to listen only to FRS,
GMRS, ham, AM, or FM radios. According to the FCC,
operate means transmit or broadcast. No license is
required to operate FRS radios. A license is required to
operate a FRS/GMRS radio in GMRS mode in the
United States. No GMRS license is required in Canada.

No test is required to obtain the GMRS license.
You simply go to the FCC website universal licensing
system [L003]
http://wireless.fcc.gov/uls/index.htm?job=home The
ULS radio service code for GMRS is ZA. I used the
word "simply" in a facetious manner.

You must be an adult (over 18) and pay the $85
application fee. The license is good for five years. After
completing the application, you will be assigned a FCC
Registration Number (FRN). The FRN, your call sign,
and your registration information are available to the
public online. The license is broader than most. One
GMRS license covers you and all members (any age) of

your family. Neither the FCC nor the public knows who or how many they are. Do not be a bubble-pack pirate, get a license.

Other Walkie-talkie Considerations

When you are using the walkie-talkie, everyone in the immediate area can hear any incoming transmissions. It may be to your advantage to be quiet whether just being courteous, trying not to disturb a game animal, or trying not to give away your position to a bad guy. Many walkie-talkies have an earpiece capability. Normally this goes into only one ear, freeing up the other ear to listen to your surrounding environment.

Walkie-talkies are push-to-talk (PTT). Depress a button on the side of the walkie-talkie and speak directly into the microphone built into the radio next to the speaker to transmit. This operation requires the use of at least one hand. It also requires considerable movement letting everyone around you know you are using a walkie-talkie. Some radios can use a combination earpiece and microphone. The microphone is clipped on your outside clothing and is remote from the actual walkie-talkie which may be in your inside pocket. The microphone is operated by a small silent button.

Some radios are virtually hands free. These walkie-talkies use voice activated transmission (VOX). When the microphone (wherever the location) detects sound, the transmission is activated until a period of silence is detected. Even some bubble-pack walkie-talkies have VOX capability. Adjustments are available to change things such as sensitivity and time delays.

Some walkie-talkies have NOAA weather alerts built in. This allows you to listen to forecasts and be alerted to potential weather problems. If you are planning on using the walkie-talkies outside, you may want to make sure they have some type of water or moisture protection. Another useful feature is "Direct Call." Direct call allows you to contact, or alert, an individual person or select group within your communication group.

Real Life Walkie-talkie Recommendation

Do your own research but here is the *Real Life Prepper* recommendation for walkie-talkies. Buy the Midland GXT1050VP4 "Up to 36 Mile Two-Way Radio." A two camouflage radio package comes with a pair of boom microphone headsets for the manufacturer's suggested retail price of $99.99. Best of all, it has five animal sound call alerts: cougar, duck, crow, wolf, and turkey. What more could you ask for?

Non-Midland walkie-talkies do not normally have the Midland extra, pre-configured channels. Nor do they normally have 104 DCS choices for privacy codes. If you want to operate with a certain, but not complete, level of privacy, your group can use one of the not so common privacy channels. Spies with the same privacy codes will be able to listen in on your conversations. Most folks will not be able to.

Short Wave Radio

Some serious preppers say that getting a ham radio license is the single best communications step you can take. Short wave radio and ham radio although not identical, are treated as virtually identical terms. You do not have to get a ham license in order to listen to short wave radio broadcasts. Many portable AM/FM radios also have a shortwave band where you can listen to both domestic and international news and information.

One good example of a listen only radio is the Sony ICF-SW7600GR AM/FM Shortwave World Band Receiver with Single Side Band Reception radio. It is AA operated with an optional AC adapter. It receives

AM, FM, Short Wave (SW), Medium Wave (MW), and Long Wave (LW). The built-in scan function is similar to the scan function for your radio in the car. It finds the next broadcasting station. It is not a "scanner."

If you decide you want to transmit, you need to get a ham license. The first or lowest level license is called the Technician License. The best source of information starts out from the American Radio Relay League (ARRL) [L005] http://www.arrl.org/. This is easier than it sounds. You do not have to know Morse Code. You do not have to be a nerd, a techie, or even an adult. They tell you all of the possible questions and answers in advance. The written, multiple choice test is 35 questions chosen randomly from the bank of the known 250 possible questions. ARRL puts out their own Ham Radio License Manual [L006] http://www.arrl.org/shop/Ham-Radio-License-Manual-Revised-2nd-Edition/ that includes practice exam software. The question bank changes on June 30, 2014 so make sure you get the correct edition. Practice exams and study guides are all over the internet and yes, there is an app for that. Try *Ham Radio Study* for Android phones.

While we are on the subject of smartphone apps, another useful app is *Scanner Radio*. It allows you to receive audio from over 4,000 police, fire, ambulance, and other emergency broadcasters over your smartphone. In fact, you can choose the area being scanned by geography rather than being limited to your antenna and local transmissions with conventional scanners. Other smartphone apps can turn your phone into a ham radio requiring you to have a FCC license to transmit.

Scanners
If you recall the "S" channel on the Motorola

TalkAbout, you will remember it was a scanning channel. When the walkie-talkie was on the "S" channel, it would scan the other ten channels (for that radio) and receive on those other channels when there was a broadcast. This scanning channel is not the same as a commonly known "scanner."

A scanner is useful to you if you want to listen to emergency broadcasts in your area. Police dispatchers, Emergency Management Agencies, hospitals, fire departments, and other folks use radios for communication. A scanner can be configured to constantly monitor radio traffic on selected frequencies. Once the scanner detects traffic, it stops scanning and delivers the audio to you. When the traffic stops, the scanner resumes its monitoring of the selected frequencies. There is no transmission from you or any license required for a scanner.

Scanners come in two styles, cheap and expensive. Actually there are many different types. Some are handheld and some are base units. Some are analog and some are digital. Some are easy to use and some are hard to use. Some you can program from the controls and some you have to use a PC to program.

RLP recommends you start out small, and then grow if you want to. Scanners can get expensive and technology is always changing. It can get irritating to listen to ambulance traffic and the local plumber dispatcher off and on all day long. The scanner you initially purchase may not be compatible with the systems used by the municipality you are trying to monitor. The highest customer rated scanner from Amazon is the Uniden BCDD996XT that retails for $499.99. It would be a $500 mistake if you found out you do not like that scanner or that you would rather carry it around in the car. There is a lot to learn.

One of the great sites to learn from is [L007] http://www.radioreference.com/. RadioReference.com has the world's largest database of frequencies. It includes links to other sites where you can learn more than you wanted to or need to know.

One of the things you need to know about is the FCC rule regarding narrowbanding. To be most effective, your scanner should be able to handle narrowband transmissions. Whereas radio channels used to be 25 kHz wide, they will soon be 12.5 kHz wide allowing for more channels. Your scanner needs to be selective enough to distinguish between channels.

Another key concept is trunking. You need to know whether your municipality uses analog or digital trunking. A scanner that only does analog trunking cannot listen in on digital trunking systems. A digital trunking capable scanner costs roughly twice as much as an analog only trunking capable scanner.

The third key concept is whether or not any agencies that you are trying to monitor use encryption and whether your scanner can decrypt the communications.

RLP recommends you do a little research before you buy even your first scanner. [L008] http://www.hamuniverse.com/scanner.html teaches you some basics and gives you some audio samples of what a scanner can do. Most folks who complain about scanners have a common problem. They can be hard to use (program). Ham Universe is going to point you to a pre-programmed scanner. [L009] http://www.dxing.com/selscan.htm is a little less verbose and more technical. If you like pictures with your text, try [L010] http://www.wikihow.com/Choose-a-Scanner-Radio. Another resource [L011] http://www.policescanners.net/ can give you specific

product recommendations based on your OP AREA
(that is prepper terminology for where you live, work,
and play).

Other Listen Only Radios

Many folks only listen to their radios in their
vehicles. If there is a tornado warning and you are
huddling in your basement, you may want to have a
portable radio with you to listen to emergency reports. If
the electricity is out, you will have to rely on battery
operated radios. If you have not been a *Real Life
Prepper*, your batteries are either missing or discharged.
One alternative is a solar powered radio. They do not
work that well in your basement, in the dark. Another
alternative is a self-powered or hand crank radio.

One good example of this type of radio is the
Eton American Red Cross ARCFR160WXR Microlink
Self-Powered AM/FM/NOAA Weather Radio. In
addition to the radio functions, it also has a flashlight
and USB phone charger connection. Use the hand crank
or built-in solar cell to charge the internal Ni-NH battery
and then use the Eton as a flashlight, cell phone charger,
or radio. At only $40 retail, it is cheap and effective
enough to get one for each vehicle and one for the
house.

Cell Phone

Cell phones are ubiquitous. Everyone knows
how to use them. Or do they? In an emergency, the cell
phones towers may be inoperable or all of the available
bandwidth (lines) may be full. Many folks have smart
phones allowing for texting (instant messaging) and
email. It is much more likely that a text message will get
through in an emergency when a voice call may not.

All of your family members should have at least
one contact in their cell phone. The contact known as
"ICE" or "In Case of Emergency" will probably be the

first one called if someone gets your phone off of your unconscious body. It may be best to have more than one ICE contact in your phone. The first ICE contact can be your close family member while your second ICE contact may be a friend or relative not in the immediate area. Sometimes long distance lines work better than local lines. And the out-of-town contact may be in a better position to coordinate other communications.

If you are not interested in a cell phone contract, you need to think about buying a prepaid cell phone package. These are available from stores such as Best Buy or Walmart. For instance, a T-Mobile Prepaid – Samsung No-Contract "t139" can be had for $29.99 from Best Buy. A T-Mobile $30 refill card costs, surprisingly, $30. You do not necessarily have to activate it right away. Some folks call these phones "burners." They pay cash and throw them away when they are finished.

The Emergency Management Agency (EMA) of most states provide a no cost application for your smartphone that alerts you in case of bad weather. For instance, the Alabama Saf-T-Net weather alert program is available at [L004] http://alabamasaftnet.com/.

The American Red Cross has two free smart phone applications. One is a Hurricane App and the other is a First Aid App. Another free smart phone application is available from Pacific Disaster Center (PDC). Disaster Alert that covers hurricane, earthquake, flood, marine, storm, and manmade disasters.

Communications Plan

Believe me, this is not overkill. Even a single sheet of paper containing your communications plan for your family is a useful addition to your preparation notebook. The communications plan should include the priorities for your communications. As much as a communications plan can be useful for your family, it is critical for your mutual assistance group. This communication plan is similar to the plans you may have for your business or for your project but they are not the same. This type of communications plan allows you to stay in contact with each other when everyone else around you is losing their head. It might be a good idea to have a shorthand communications plan on a card given to each family or group member.

For your family, the communications plan might be really simple. Typically it will be part of your regular emergency plan. You probably can control your family's acquisitions a little better than you can control purchases in your mutual assistance group. Buying the same radios or at least radios from the same manufacturer will eliminate most of those possible incompatibilities. Then you decide on frequencies or channels you should use in what situations.

For your mutual assistance group (MAG), things get more complicated. You will have old radios, new radios, different model radios, and most importantly, multiple personalities. The communications plan for a MAG will probably have to include frequencies as well as channels. It may also include different strategies for different needs such as logistics, medical, and security.

LIGHTING

Most people do not like to be awake in the dark. Certainly they do not like to read, cook, or eat in the dark. Lighting is a critical part of real life prepping. Power failures do not just come as a result of the zombie apocalypse or an electromagnetic pulse (EMP) attack. Depending on the weather and where you live, a power outage may be an everyday occurrence. When the power goes out, usually the lights go out.

There are other issues associated with lighting that can actually cause your regular life to suffer an event that is harmful to your health and happiness. As a *Real Life Prepper*, you need to be prepared to manage those events. Sometimes RLP believes that the purpose of the Environmental Protection Agency (EPA) is to increase costs and do significant damage to our environment. Just consider the so-called low flow toilets and the Compact Fluorescent Light bulb (CFL). CFLs are inherently dangerous. Take a look at what the EPA tells you to do in case you break one in your home. If you research more, you will find that some folks recommend even more extreme measures including cutting the exposed section out of your carpet. Prepare for a breakage in the manner that makes most sense to you. If you elect to use CFLs, print out the instructions for handling a break [L097] http://www2.epa.gov/cfl/cleaning-broken-cfl and have the needed cleanup materials available in a kit. It sounds like the EPA has brought a potential miniature zombie apocalypse right into your living room without you even knowing about it.

As you prepare for lighting outages, you need to characterize them in order to manage them. For instance, a 30-second lighting outage is probably not going to convince you to invest a lot of resources to prepare. For the purposes of this discussion, let's not directly consider short-term, medium-term, and long-term lighting outages because they may have different meanings to you. Rather, let's discuss lighting outages for hours, for days, and for weeks. Your preparations may overlap but they will still have distinctive requirements. Considerations include but are not limited to: flashlights, kerosene lanterns, candles, solar, LEDs, and blackout curtains.

Lighting Outage for Hours (short-term)

At your office, at church, and at the movie theater, the building managers have configured battery operated lighting so that you will be able to see even if the primary lights go out for just a few seconds. This is probably not really in the scope and control of the *Real Life Prepper*. Or is it? The automatic flashlight described in the Security chapter probably provides all of the short-term, emergency, battery backup lighting you need for an outage only lasting a matter of minutes or hours.

RLP highly recommends you rely only on flashlights for lighting outages lasting no more than a few hours. Everything else becomes too much of a hassle and manifests diminishing returns on your resources.

Lighting Outage for Days (medium-term)

For a lighting outage lasting just a matter of days, you still want to consider just using flashlights. Candles are an option but do provide significant risk in the area of potential fires. If managed correctly, the candles will provide ambiance along with some lighting. But be aware of the inherent dangers of candles and flames. Remember, you really only need lighting when it is dark. The flashlights will not be on all the time but will be readily available. Candles are just not that readily available on a moment's notice. Candles are hard to carry around and hard to shine into a dark space. Batteries are the key to providing lighting during an outage lasting more than a few hours. With no spare batteries and no way to recharge the batteries you have, your options diminish rapidly.

Lighting Outage for Weeks (long-term)

For a lighting outage lasting more than just a few days, the *Real Life Prepper* must make some tough decisions. Your flashlight batteries will not last. They will need to be replaced or recharged. With no electricity, you may have a tough time recharging the batteries.

Many *Doomsday Preppers* are already operating on 12-volt lights. When the grid goes down, they are perfectly prepared to continue operating their own lights on their battery bank. Of course they need to keep their battery bank charged up. The *Real Life Prepper* probably does not have 12-volt lights available or installed. However, many recreational vehicles and campers have dual systems that operate either 110-volt lighting or 12-volt lighting. RLP has hunted at a camp where the only source of power was a propane generator. The generator kept the battery bank charged up. The 12-volt DC battery bank was not used directly but rather used an inverter to convert the electrical energy into 120 volt AC power and thus used regular 110 volt lighting.

The *Real Life Prepper* may want to seriously consider using kerosene lanterns during a power and lighting outage lasting more than a few days. A glass "oil lamp" is different than a kerosene lantern. But both will need fuel, wicks, and management. Manage your flashlights and flashlight batteries as they will continue to be useful.

Light Discipline

Dark is the opposite of light. When RLP was in the Navy, we took great pains to keep light from the darkness. There were two reasons for this. First, if you were trying to see in the dark and your eyes were exposed to much light; you lost your night vision. We read and operated equipment using red light so we would still be able to see contacts (other ships) that might present a danger to ours. Sailors were not even allowed to use a match on the bridge to light their own cigarettes. Second, a bad guy could see light "leaking" out of our ship from miles away.

The *Real Life Prepper* can apply these same principles to his or her own home when there is a lighting outage. You are reducing your own capabilities and limited resources if you keep one part of your house so bright that you cannot really see in the other part of the house without the same amount of light. After an extended power and lighting outage, if yours is the only house around with light streaming out of the windows, it will attract attention. This may not be the position you want your family to be in. There are bad guys out there and they now know you have power, lights, and supplies.

RLP has trouble sleeping if outside lights penetrate the Bat Cave. Some folks have even implemented blackout curtains to keep outside lights from penetrating the Fortress of Solitude. Those same blackout curtains also keep inside light from leaking into the environment. Purchasing and testing blackout curtains are things that need to be done well before they are actually needed. A thin wool blanket is not as much of a blackout curtain as you think it might be. Act like one of those Civil Defense inspectors in the old movies before you are satisfied. You need to consider how they are going to be mounted, how they are going to be traversed, and how you are going to keep them safe from fire.

Flashlights and Batteries

The RLP family frequently houses missionaries traveling back into the United States. We always make sure they are prepared as necessary for a lighting outage if we are not at home. Recently MrsRLP asked a young missionary if he knew where a flashlight was in case the lights went out. The response to MrsRLP was simply, "You are the flashlight people. They are everywhere!" And he is right. A handy, available, and working flashlight can keep you sane and comfortable. RLP is actually comfortable and embarrassed at the same time about the availability of good flashlights in the RLP family home and vehicles.

Flashlights and Batteries (rechargeable and disposable)

Flashlights and flashlight batteries have evolved over time. Many of us can remember C-cell and even clunky D-cell batteries. As flashlights thinned down and lightened up, they went to an adapter with three AAA or single stacks of AA or AAA. Bulbs used to be incandescent (generate lots of heat, require lots of power, break easy), then went to LED (less heat, less power requirements, less light, last longer), and have now evolved to CREE LEDs (less heat, less power requirements, more light, last longer). You will recognize the CREE LED when you look through the lens – with the light off, of course – and see a small square that looks like a circuit board. The CREE LED flashlights can hurt your eyes.

Flashlights use batteries. Batteries fail when you need them the most. I have not had real good experiences with batteries, including brand name, new batteries with an expiration date way into the future. Some "tactical" flashlights now use a CR123A battery (or two) because they have a high power density. These batteries are fairly expensive and are not available in every store. Sometimes called a "camera battery," they are disposable, lithium, three (3) volt, and have a typical capacity of 1500 mAh. There is a bigger, Li-ion version that is rechargeable but at only 700 mAh. RLP has never seen the rechargeable version.

You need some perspective here. The term "mAh" stands for milli-ampere hour. It is a measure of how much power is stored. Lots of mAh in a small package makes for a high power density. Use it to compare one battery to the next.

Please indulge me here. RLP's inner engineer just had to be heard. This may be technical but it is good stuff. My new "go to" flashlights use CREE LEDs and a new type of battery called an 18650. This is nominally a 3.7 volt, Li-ion battery that is rechargeable. Note that these require a special charger to be safe. Some of the 18650 batteries have built-in circuitry (makes them bigger) to protect the battery and the consumer. The first two digits of the designation estimate the diameter, the last three digits estimate the height (in tenths) – both in millimeters. The CR123A is 17mm in diameter, the 18650 is 18.6mm in diameter (close enough to 18). The CR123A is 34.5mm high, the 18650 is 68mm tall. It would have been 65.0mm high without the protective circuitry. In other words, the 18650 is roughly the same diameter but twice the height of the CR123A. Here is the good news. The 18650 is rechargeable but has a capacity between 2200 and 3400 mAh (three to five times the capacity of the rechargeable CR123A); it has a higher power density.

RLP highly recommends you not scrimp on flashlight batteries. You can get them fairly cheap from Amazon where there are four generic 3000 mAh 18650s for $8. On the other hand, the four 3400 mAh Orbtronic circuit protected batteries go for $64. The prices are all over the map. The RLP family relies on flashlights for emergency purposes. RLP decided on the Orbtronic [L071] http://www.Amazon.com/gp/product/B00CAD6AUE/ref=oh_details_o07_s00_i02?ie=UTF8&psc=1

TaoTronics Thorlite Review

[L072]http://www.amazon.com/gp/product/B00AXVNOHM/ref=oh_details_o05_s00_i02?ie=UTF8&psc=1 RLP wanted to like this flashlight, bad. It is packaged very nicely with spare O-rings, a great lanyard, a carrying case, and instructions. It does not come with a battery but that is clear enough in the description. It is silver and black which is bad or good, depending on what you want. RLP did not notice any significantly sharp edges as noted in another review. The stainless steel strike bezel can be used for defense and can be screwed off (leaving exposed threads) if you do not like it. The 18650 battery purchased separately fit perfectly, highlighting quality fit and finish. RLP was so excited about the flashlight, we bought two. One was dead on arrival. RLP could never get it to work. The second light worked fine, if you could get the tail piece switch to operate. It took a little getting used to but RLP could operate it with some difficulty as compared to the Vizeri Compact Tactical Cree LED and Afunta WF-502B CREE XM-L T6 flashlights purchased at the same time. The problem was that MrsRLP could initially not get the TaoTronics to operate consistently without a considerable struggle. The reason for paying "high-dollar" for a high-quality flashlight is to make sure MrsRLP can easily operate it in an emergency. TaoTronics later made everything right.

You may also want to check out the Nighthawk Ultralight flashlights [L074] http://www.nighthawklights.com for a small, high quality flashlight.

Brite Strike Lights [L099}

http://www.amazon.com/gp/product/B007T3Q1UY/ref= oh_details_o06_s01_i00?ie=UTF8&psc=1 are an innovative way to have a stick-on, temporary flashlight to illuminate equipment or people. Since they are flat and self-adhesive, they are extremely convenient. Consider using them to identify and keep track of equipment and children.

There is no truth to the rumor that RLP actually stands for "really lazy paranoid." However, I tend to want to do things efficiently and because I am concerned. The RLP family home has more than one safe room. It could become a burden to make sure the flashlights in the potentially dark rooms always have charged batteries. Instead, RLP settled for the efficient route. Hybrid Light [L101] http://hybridlight.com/products/ makes a solar rechargeable flashlight we just sit in the windowsill. When the sun is out, the rechargeable batteries recharge. They maintain enough power to sustain a good light even when overcast for several days. They are relatively cheap, durable, and just plain work. RLP highly recommends them.

Infinite Non-battery Lights

Yes, there is such a thing! And they are not expensive. No batteries, no bulbs, no electricity and they are reusable forever. RLP would not use them to do surgery but they seem bright when your eyes are adjusted to the dark. Check out the UVPaqlite [137] https://www.uvpaqlite.com/ and at least consider their trial pack.

Kerosene lanterns

These types of lanterns are known by several different names such as oil lamps, hurricane lamps, railroad lanterns, or Dietz lanterns. Be aware that some are not even safe for use in the home. All require training, consumable supplies, and have inherent risks. Even the type of kerosene you use is a major factor. Paraffin in the United Kingdom is kerosene; paraffin in the United States is liquid candle wax and is not suitable for most of the lamps we are talking about. Clear K-1 kerosene with a flash point of 124 to 150 degrees is recommended for outside use. Standard Lamp Oil or Synthetic Kerosene is recommended by Kirkman for indoor use. Please check out their website for more specific recommendations. If you have a kerosene space heater, it is probably configured to use K-1 kerosene.

W.T. Kirkman [L075] http://www.lanternnet.com/ provides a substantial amount of information about kerosene and other lanterns. Surprisingly, they even sell some made in the United States. For use in your home, you need to understand the fundamental differences between the Cold-Blast, Hot-Blast, and Dead-Flame lanterns. If you want to breathe clean air, these differences are critical. Decorative lighting is substantially different than necessity and utility lighting. Although you may end up purchasing your lanterns from Amazon or Walmart, knowledge is weightless. Know what you are doing before you risk your family's life. Copyrighted text by W.T. Kirkman used with permission, courtesy of www.lanternnet.com.

Candles

Candles have been discussed at length in the Fire Protection chapter. RLP believes that in general, the risks of a fire from candles in a stressful situation outweigh the benefits of the ambiance and provided light. However, properly managed candles with appropriate safety measures and holders should not be totally discounted. Candles are not for children nor should they be carried around like a flashlight, or even a lantern.

Solar

In addition to solar backup power for other devices, Goal Zero [L098] http://www.goalzero.com/ makes a high quality line of solar lighting devices. Remember that when the sun is out, you probably do not need that much extra lighting. This will require energy storage devices to collect the solar energy in batteries to be supplied to the low energy LED lights when it is dark. Goal Zero evens make a cool LUNA LED strip that runs off the USB port on your laptop. Of course, Goal Zero also makes the battery storage devices.

Cheap outdoor sidewalk solar lighting available from Walmart or Lowes is also a viable option. These devices can just lie around outside during the day and be used in your home at night like a torch. Did RLP mention they were cheap? A small solar LED pathway lighting garden or farm on your deck or patio can be unobtrusive and ready to go on a moment's notice.

Cheap LED string lighting [L100] http://www.amazon.com/gp/product/B003V8IR2Q/ref=o h_details_o02_s01_i00?ie=UTF8&psc=1 can be charged up in the daytime and deployed in your home during the darkness. The solar charger even works through your window. RLP recommends using all blue lights to protect your night vision. You do not have to tell anyone they were designed for Christmas decorations.

Harbor Freight sells an inexpensive 45-watt solar panel kit [L102] http://www.harborfreight.com/solar-panel-kit-45-watt-68751.html and it can be even cheaper when on sale or with a coupon. This is a starter kit that will not directly work for the *Real Life Prepper*. It must be setup and operational before it can be used. Most importantly, there is no place to store the energy for when it gets dark. There are no included batteries or a power inverter. However, RLP highly recommends the kit as a place to start, learn, and experiment. It even comes with 12-volt lights!

Epica [L103] http://www.amazon.com/gp/product/B00CZDT30S/ref=oh_details_o09_s00_i01?ie=UTF8&psc=1 makes a flashlight, USB charger, and radio that charges from the sun or from a hand crank. It is even rubberized and waterproof. RLP highly recommends this type of radio for your home, car, or for a Christmas gift.

HEATING

The *Real Life Prepper* approach to heating preparations is fundamentally going to be based on the length of the power grid or heating outage. Some of the things you need to look at are your location and your climate. Part of the RLP family lives in an apartment on a tropical island. They have no heat at all in their apartment but still get cold.

Heating Outage for Hours (short-term)

Sometimes things are just not worth the effort. For a short-term heating outage, RLP recommends you just consider toughing it out. It is unlikely that anyone other than very small children will suffer any adverse impact from a heating outage lasting only a few hours. RLP recommends putting on a hat and jacket. If it gets really cold, break out some extra blankets and snuggle. RLP recommends you acquire some extra blankets that might serve a double purpose but not necessarily be the same blankets you use on a regular nightly basis. An electric space heater such as the parabolic heater discussed below can resolve most other issues as long as there is power available. Most modern conventional fire places do more harm than good and end up pumping the useful heat from your house into the neighborhood sky.

Heating Outage for Days (medium-term)

Depending on the severity of the cold and expectations for recovery, the *Real Life Prepper* needs to take additional steps to keep warm. These additional steps may not be easily taken if you have not prepared properly. Of course, jackets, hats, and blankets can still be leveraged. Additional steps can be difficult to take in the cold and in the dark. Without electricity for a space heater, the *Real Life Prepper* is probably looking at a kerosene space heater. During one extended electrical outage and without a kerosene space heater, the RLP family moved into a hotel. Fortunately, the hotel had power.

Heating Outage for Weeks (long-term)

If your home is without heat and electricity on a long-term basis, the local hotel is mostly likely suffering from the same fate. You need power, you need fire, or you need a kerosene space heater. A camp fire in the middle of your living room may keep you warm but is probably not in your best interest. Although some folks do heat or supplement their regular heat with a wood stove, the typical *Real Life Prepper* is not prepared with a wood stove or enough firewood to maintain comfortable temperatures for an extended period. Natural gas may or may not be available to your home even if electricity is not. Some fireplace designs with built-in heating units may be able to keep you warm. Now is not the time to purchase a kerosene space heater, kerosene, spare wicks, fuel transfer devices, learn how to manage your heater, or if anyone in your family has difficulty with the resultant fumes. Your family should be trained and practiced in kerosene heater operations before you need the heat.

Another alternative is to temporarily downsize your living spaces. Try living in a smaller number of rooms so that you do not have to heat the entire house. You might think about using an electric space heater powered from your generator on a limited basis. Consider your previous investments into community and how you might share resources.

Using natural gas, wood, or kerosene in your home to supply heat brings with it the risk of carbon monoxide poisoning. RLP recommends you install carbon monoxide detectors now in the areas you are most likely to use those types of heaters. You should also have the detectors installed in your garage even though you may not use those heaters in your garage.

Portable propane heaters, such as those made by Mr. Heater [L140] http://www.mrheater.com/ProductFamily.aspx?catid=41 are not really suitable for inside the home. The propane supply tank is not suitable for use inside the home nor do most homes provide adequate ventilation or combustion air. They do have a purpose and they work great when used properly.

Electric Parabolic Heater

RLP loves the way Costco does marketing. For a long time, Costco featured a parabolic heater, like the Presto [L139] http://prestoheater.com/presto-heatdish-parabolic-heater-plus-footlight that beamed heat onto passing customers. Every customer stopped to bask in the warmth. People just like to be warm. An electric parabolic heater like this actually warms up the person rather than a space. If you can imagine the Costco warehouse environment, you can see how this was a more effective demonstration than a space heater and would not carry the same impact as a regular electric or kerosene space heater. The RLP family ended up with more than one. For a heating outage where power is still available, this directed type of heat may meet all of your needs.

COOLING

Whoa now! We are starting to fool around with a great American expectation. Our great grandparents did not have to live without air conditioning. Why should we? With the exception of small children, expectant mothers, some sick people, and some elderly only under certain conditions, a cooling outage presents more of a discomfort than a danger to health and well being. Most of us can get by without artificial cooling.

Cooling Outage for Hours (short-term)

RLP recommends that for a cooling outage lasting no more than just a few hours, you tough it out. Even more so than for a short-term heating outage, it is probably not worth the effort to prepare for or implement a solution.

Cooling Outage for Days (medium-term)

RLP recommends that you use your windows for a cooling outage that lasts for days. There could be some significant considerations before you actually decide to use your windows. The first consideration is security. When your windows are unlocked and open, you increase the risk that a bad guy might decide to enter your house illegally and do you harm. How are you going to maintain security with unlocked windows? The second consideration is whether or not your windows actually work. In many modern homes, the windows have never actually been operated or they have been painted over. Operate and test yours now while things are still comfortable. The third consideration is bugs. Many windows do not have screens at all. The mosquitoes may bother you more than a little sweat. Window fans that blow out have fallen out of vogue but there are not many mosquitoes that can fly upstream against the blast of a fan. Obviously electricity must be available to operate the window fan.

Ceiling fans (still needing electricity) can lower or raise the felt temperature of a room considerably. RLP recommends you install ceiling fans at least in all bedrooms. Most are bi-directional. Blow down to cool and up to make best use of the heat in the room.

At some expense, RLP highly recommends you investigate Crimsafe [L141] http://www.crimsafe.com/ security screens. They satisfy all of my requirements except for being free. They are fantastic!

Cooling Outage for Weeks (long-term)
The *Real Life Prepper* solution for a long-term cooling outage is to restructure your life. Without electricity and a working cooling system, you are going to sweat. RLP recommends that you purchase a 110-volt window air conditioning unit for backup purposes if your problem is your central cooling system and not your power. Try the fit and operation in your bedroom before you need to deploy it. RLP would easily run a generator just to supply electricity to the window unit in the bedroom.

For rooms that do not have standard double hung windows that can accommodate a window air conditioning unit, there is still an alternative. Many companies manufacture a standalone, portable air conditioning unit that uses flexible ducting (hoses) rather than having the unit rest on the window sill. These kinds of units are the kind you see being used in computer rooms or for spot cooling.

BUG OUT OR BUG IN

A lot of prepper controversy swirls around the idea of whether you should bug out when the schumer hits the proverbial fan or if you should shelter in place (bug in). Real life people cannot normally afford to purchase, maintain, and protect two households. The general consensus is that if you have a Bug Out Location (BOL), it is better to live there fulltime then to have to get there when the balloon goes up. For a retiree, this may make great sense. RLP thinks that it may be very difficult to balance life's activities and then still get everything you need at home to your separate BOL in an emergency situation.

However, you should have a backup plan. If a tornado, hurricane, fire, meteor strike, or terrorist strike takes out your home, you should have a plan where to go, what you need to bring, and how you are going to get there. Your BOL may simply be a friend's or a relative's house. Their BOL may be your house.

You still need a bag – or two – or more. RLP highly recommends you establish and maintain at least two bags. The most important is your Get Home Bag (GHB). You should have a GHB in each vehicle. You might think about a Bug Out Bag (BOB) for your home.

Get Home Bag (GHB)

A GHB is a common sense approach that gives you some security and comfort when something happens to you out of the ordinary and you are not at home. You do not want to have to necessarily rely on the kindness of others to get you home. Many of you ladies dress up for work. You may wear a suit and heels. Do you really want to walk four miles in your heels, in the snow, uphill to just get home if you run out of gas or get a flat tire?

RLP recommends a non-descript and not shiny backpack rather than a hand carry bag. You want your hands free to use, to steady yourself, or to defend yourself. This means the backpack should be properly adjusted and tested ahead of time.

Some folks live in a jurisdiction that cares more about government control than the safety and welfare of its citizens. Others work in an office that does not allow tools of liberty either in the office or even in the parking lot (like the U.S. Post Office). If you decide to provision your GHB in a fashion that could violate some of those rules, there are alternatives. Sometimes there are climate controlled storage facilities near your office where you could stash or cache your GHB and perhaps even a bicycle. Then of course, you could just do what you think is best for you and ignore the progressives who think they know better than you do. Then again, they have probably not read *Real Life Prepper*.

RLP thinks that each GHB will be unique for each individual but will share some commonalities. Therefore, we will touch on the philosophy and then list some suggested items that you can tailor to your own needs.

Bug Out Bag (BOB)

In a room full of 99 preppers, you will have at least 120 different opinions about the contents of a properly equipped BOB. Several may even have their small, fanny pack BOBs around their waists whenever you see them. Their BOB or kit can be as small as an Altoids can or be as large as a trunk.

Philosophy of GHB and BOB

The contents of your GHB and BOB will vary with your size, your training, your environment, and your expectations. If you expect to have to subsist solely from your bag for a week rather than half a day, clearly the contents will differ. If you are an 89 pound ex-librarian woman, your bag will probably be different than if you are a 250 pound ex-Marine male.

Think about where you are going to engage your GHB and where you are heading. Normally your GHB will be at your office and/or in your vehicle. How far is it from your office to your home? What do you wear to work? What is the climate and what are the road or trail conditions?

Think about how far it is to your BOL. Will you carry your BOB on your back or will your roll it? How long will it take to get from your home to your BOL? What conditions will you face in your travels? Can you afford to stand out or do you want to blend in?

The following two lists are meant to be suggestions and not check lists. They should help guide your own thought processes.

Suggested Contents of GHB
- Leather gloves
- Small first aid kit
- A few plastic garbage bags
- A couple of flares
- Two flashlights
- Paper maps of area
- Good folding knife
- Water
- Life straw or other water purifier like a filtered Berkey Sports bottle
- Self-contained eye glass repair kit
- Matches and lighters
- Snack or power bar
- Good walking shoes
- Good socks
- Good hat
- Expandable baton

- Tested and proven firearm with gun belt, holster, ammunition, and spare magazines
- Change of clothes
- Writing pad and implement
- Some cash (FRNs)
- Some toilet paper or equivalent

Suggested Contents of BOB

- Leather gloves
- Medium size first aid kit
- A few plastic garbage bags
- A flare gun with flares
- Two flashlights
- Paper maps of area with marked routes
- Good folding knife
- Water
- Life straw or other water purifier like a MSR
- Self-contained eye glass repair kit
- Paracord
- Matches and lighters
- Biolite stove
- Snacks or power bars
- Spare eye glasses
- Sufficient meals for trip, MRE or freeze dried
- Good walking shoes
- Good socks, as many as necessary
- Good hat
- Expandable baton
- Tested and proven firearm with gun belt, holster, ammunition, and spare magazines
- Change of clothes
- Writing pad and implement
- Some cash (FRNs)
- Roll of junk silver dimes
- Sleeping bag
- Tent or equivalent shelter
- Some toilet paper or equivalent
- Emergency blanket

TRANSPORTATION

Both the *Doomsday Prepper* and the *Real Life Prepper* need to be transported sometime somewhere. This can range from a rather inexpensive proposition (your feet) to an expensive venture (your vehicle). Regardless, it requires serious consideration.

Vehicles

Like all good Southern boys, RLP has a 4x4 pickup. Perfect for hunting, it may not be the best choice for the everyday commute to the office. As a suburban *Real Life Prepper* vehicle, the pickup is a necessity and has hauled around its share of lumber and pine straw. A *Doomsday Prepper* may be able to purchase and maintain a dedicated BOV but RLP is not made of money. The other RLP family car was the type of standard sedan that sits in the street or garage of every suburbanite. RLP had every intention of using the 4x4 pickup as the vehicle of choice if tough traveling conditions arose.

God is gracious and merciful. About the same time RLP was thinking about good, tough transportation in case of an emergency and it was time to replace the sedan, MrsRLP was partially out of commission. RLP was able to stumble over the right solution quite by accident.

You have either already read about or will read about the freak 2014 ice and snow storm that devastated Alabama and made traveling so difficult. That day and night, every Southern boy in the state was out on the road in their own 4x4 pickup trying to get home, to work, or to help someone out of a jam. The RLP family was riding in the accidental purchase since the RLP family 4x4 pickup was at home. RLP has since renamed the accidental purchase "The Beast."

Subaru uses a technology called symmetrical All Wheel Drive (AWD). The Beast is the Subaru Outback with AWD and standard high ground clearance that RLP stumbled on while MrsRLP was temporarily out of commission. During that freak storm, RLP passed literally hundreds of 4x4 pickups, tens of emergency vehicles, thousands of sedans, and even a deployed National Guard deuce-and-a-half trying to clear the roads. All of these other vehicles were either stuck in the middle of the road, wrecked on the side of the road, or generally just in the way. The Beast just needed a clear path to home and literally was never in danger of getting stuck because of the weather. RLP believes that the Subaru, particularly the Outback, is the perfect vehicle for the *Real Life Prepper*. The RLP family is in total agreement that it has been our favorite vehicle even when not considering emergency transportation. The 4x4 pickup is still much better at hauling lumber and harvested whitetail deer.

RLP can be a creature of habit. In fact, I feel naked and exposed when I even step outside of the house front door and am not dressed properly. This includes when I am in The Beast or 4x4 pickup. I need to have my keys, my wallet, my pistol, and my knife. You can readily identify other guys with my type of personality by looking for the folding knife belt clip sticking outside of the pants pocket. Yes, I am that guy. Unfortunately, the rest of society may not agree with everything I do. Sometimes RLP must venture into government buildings or private establishments that do not appreciate fundamental constitutional rights. One of my greatest concerns is to not be able to fend for myself. It is a long walk back from the hunting camp if I misplace my keys. It is no walk back if a government bureaucrat sees my folding knife belt clip in my pocket and decides I am a threat. And of course, I want to keep everyone safe.

Back in the day, a magnetic key holder was a popular device for storing a spare key on your vehicle. Has anyone else noticed that more and more cars are actually made out of plastic now? Or that keys with a built-in security device or key fob are getting much bigger? I can pretty much guarantee you that any RLP magnetic key holder is going to end up on the side of the road where it will never be seen again. There is an alternative. Hitch Safe [L115] http://www.hitchsafe.com/ sells a mechanical combination safe that fits inside your towing receiver. The combination can be changed by the end-user and it is totally safe yet accessible from outside the vehicle. This safe is big enough to safely store the largest modern vehicle key plus other materials if you want to keep them there.

What can RLP do to keep the pistol, knife, and wallet legal and safe when necessary? RLP is an absolute fan of the very tough and very flexible FAS1 handgun safe [L042] http://fas1safe.com/ already mentioned in the Security chapter. A V-Line safe [L041] http://vlineind.com/Default.php can also be mounted below your seat and still meet your needs. If mounted inside the locked vehicle, neither does a great job of allowing you access to your keys.

Now that The Beast and the 4x4 pickup are partially equipped and fully proven, they still do not meet all of my requirements for the perfect *Real Life Prepper* vehicles. For some reason, they need gasoline to operate and they do not come with all of the gear I feel I need on an everyday basis.

Gasoline

Gasoline, gasoline treatments, and fuel transfer are covered in detail in the Energy and Power chapter. What is not covered is one of the easiest and greatest things you can do to keep prepared in your everyday life. One of the earliest and most enforced RLP family rules is that the gas gauge on any RLP vehicle cannot go below the one-quarter full level. At that level, we should be able to make it home, to a friend's or relative's house, or at least to a gas station. (If the schumer hits the fan, that rule will have to change.) Even if we make it to the gas station, they want us to pay for the gas! We have to plan for contingencies like an expired credit card, no internet connection, or a local station that does not take a credit card. Cash for gasoline stored in your vehicle is a good idea.

It has always been MrsRLP's job to carry around emergency cash. When we began this initiative, it was $20. Now $20 is only worth $10 thanks to the private central bank we call the "Federal Reserve Bank." Sometimes that $20 ends up in the wrong purse or spent on an emergency sandwich. RLP now recommends stashing dedicated cash in each vehicle so that it is accessible to the driver when needed. Each family needs to determine how much emergency gasoline cash they should store in each vehicle.

Regardless of how you pay for your gasoline or where you get it from, you still need to get it into your vehicle to make it useful. The regular gas pump nozzle at a gas station normally has no problems. But what happens if someone brings the gasoline to you? RLP has rescued many folks that had run out of gasoline on the side of the road. The design of modern vehicles has moved the gasoline tank fill inlet more and more to the side panel of the vehicle. The entrance becomes a vertical hole rather than one where you can just pour gasoline into the tank. Many modern portable poly type gas cans with EPA restrictions are incapable of being used to actually get gasoline into your vehicle's tank. They do a good job of washing off the mud and tar on the side of the vehicle.

The solution here is to use a funnel. The funnel needs to be in the vehicle, not at home, for you to be properly prepared. RLP has experimented with a number of funnels and most of them do not work properly. Depending on the design, the funnel spout can be too stiff, too large in diameter, or unable to hold open the EPA mandated flap in your vehicle tank filler opening. Remember that gasoline, like water, weighs about eight pounds per gallon. When you are attempting to fill your vehicle from a five-gallon portable tank, you will need to watch out for traffic, tilt your portable 40-pound tank properly, manage your funnel, and keep the gasoline off of your shoes. This task must be one that is proven and practiced by each driver in your household.

RLP highly recommends a galvanized metal funnel with a flexible spout. The hard but conformable spout helps you manage the funnel operation while keeping the EPA mandated flap open. Most of these types of funnels have a permanent brass or other metal screen filter in between the funnel itself and the flexible spout. The flexible spout should be at least one foot long. Make sure that the diameter is small enough to fit into your vehicle gas tank opening. Behrens manufactures one such funnel [L116] http://www.behrensmfg.com/products/by-type/funnels/ that works great. You will need to figure out how to store the funnel in your vehicle after use.

Vehicle Battery Preservation

Occasionally the *Real Life Prepper* has a need to store a vehicle that is not driven often. The battery has a good chance of not operating when it needs to. You might be tempted to put a cheap trickle charger on the battery to maintain the charge. Harbor Freight sells an inexpensive charger for around $5.00. In a pinch, that will work.

RLP recommends a battery tender similar to that supplied by [L146] http://batterytender.com/. It will "tend" your vehicle battery and potentially make it last longer as well as make it available when you need it. Although more expensive, it is worth it. The battery tender is usually available at Sam's, Costco, and Amazon.

Everyday Vehicle Kit Items

RLP has a list of items that should be in your vehicle on a normal, day-to-day basis. The hardest part of this kit is how to store it securely and keep it up-to-date. Some folks also recommend an emergency seat belt cutter and window breaker escape tool that is not part of the kit. It is extremely hard to break out any car window on purpose. If purchased, the tool must be readily accessible to the driver without having to dig around in the vehicle kit.

- Portable compressor and jump starter – this may be the one you use the most, it also usually has a built-in flashlight
- Gasoline funnel
- Emergency gasoline money
- Flashlight – keep batteries fresh
- Water – drinking and washing, can use drinking water for washing. Be aware that water bottled in standard plastic bottles can be adversely impacted by the plastic's reaction to the heat and sun. It is still useful for washing gasoline or mud off of your hands.
- Gloves – disposable, wrap the flashlight in them to keep it from rolling around
- First Aid Kit – include CPR protection
- Tire Pressure Gage
- GHB
- Pen or pencil and writing pad
- Self-contained eye glass repair kit

- A small tool kit – screw drivers, a few wrenches, small pry bar, etc. Nothing fancy here

RLP recommends a plastic tote with a lid to keep most of these items secure. It can go in your trunk and be easily removed in one piece if you get your vehicle serviced.

A larger tool kit may be appropriate to carry around in the 4x4 pickup. RLP has been stuck in the woods by himself with one wheel off of the ground. The Beast with symmetrical AWD does not suffer from that issue but it does not normally go into the woods. Eventually I hailed down a tractor to pull me the two feet to where I could get some traction. If I had a Come-Along [L120] http://www.northerntool.com/shop/tools/product_20051 1810_200511810 in the truck tool box, I could have connected to a tree and pulled myself the two feet to rescue.

Sometimes RLP just feels the need for additional tools such as a pick, axe, shovel, sledge, etc. That is a lot of stuff to carry around. Hi-Lift [L121] http://www.hiliftjack.org/hi-lift-jack-ha-500-handle-all-multi-purpose-tool makes a great portable tool kit that shares a common handle. The 4x4 pickup never leaves the garage without that kit in the bed toolbox.

Although not directly related to transportation, RLP is in love with another Hi-Lift tool. RLP purchased a cheap farm jack at a yard sale and threw it into the back of the 4x4 pickup for a trip to the hunting camp where we had to change the tires on a few campers. We tried several combinations of hydraulic and floor jacks in an attempt to change the tires. Several of the jacks broke and it took us a long time. RLP finally remembered the farm jack and we were done in just a matter of moments. The cheap farm jack immediately became a gift to one of the hunting buddies. RLP subsequently spent the money for the real thing and never regretted the purchase of a real Hi-Lift Jack [L122] http://www.hi-lift.com/hi-lift-jacks/index.html along with a spare parts kit and some accessories.

Portable Compressor and Jump Starter

These handy little devices are ubiquitous and quite cheap for the value they deliver. RLP has rescued a number of victims just by picking up the device and jump starting their car with the attached jumper cables. It was much more convenient than blocking traffic, aligning batteries, and laying out jumper cables. Just make sure you periodically charge them up.

Manual air pump

A Real *Life Prepper* is probably going to rely on the portable compressor and jump starter. A *Doomsday Prepper* will not trust only one source of compressed air so will also carry a manual air pump. RLP does not think that is necessary.

Good Shoes and Socks

Sorry ladies, you are most of the problem here. You might end up paying a high price for looking good at the office. Even with good car maintenance, plenty of gasoline and a vehicle kit, your car may break down. One flat tire may not stop you but two probably will. Many folks incorporate good walking shoes and socks into their GHB. You do not have to have new or fancy walking shoes to get to assistance or even to walk home. Just make sure they are comfortable and will meet the needs of your environment. RLP recommends you recycle an older pair of proven shoes into your vehicle kit as you will not need them very often. But when you need them, you really need them.

Maps of Your Area

Reading a map is coming to be a lost art. We live in such a technology driven world that many folks either follow their GPS or blindly commute back and forth without realizing what is around them. A paper map of your OP AREA is really cheap and might help you get out a jam. It also might be useful if you periodically reviewed the map and made some notes directly on the paper. Notes might include a meet up spot, danger areas, or safety areas that are not normally in your line of sight.

FIRE PROTECTION

Wait just a minute! How does a chapter about fire protection get into a book about real life prepping? Think about it for a minute. I can probably guess that more of us have fire insurance, a smoke detector, or at least a fire extinguisher than have made any serious preparations for the zombie apocalypse. Real life prepping is preparing for real life events. A fire is a real life event that we need to prepare for. If you have not had a fire in your home, office, or car yet, you will have.

Fire Prevention

The best way to protect you and your family from the consequences of a fire is to not have one in the first place. Back in the day, we were all taught about the fire triangle. Simplified, you need fuel, oxygen, and a heat source to have a fire. Remove any of those factors and either the fire cannot start or it will go out. RLP could recommend that you live on the surface of the moon but that is not very real life, is it?

Many folks think that candles are a good way to provide emergency lighting if the power goes out. With candles come matches, open flames, and hot wax. Properly managed, they can be a solution, but RLP does not recommend them as a first resort in a stressful situation. Most of us are not used to managing candles on a routine basis.

In a grid down situation in the winter, you will need some heat. Most likely you will have a space heater of some sort. That space heater may be fueled by kerosene. Have you practiced how to refuel, light, and manage a kerosene appliance? Have you taken steps to keep it from being tipped over? What about a kerosene lantern with a glass globe?

How are you going to heat your water and cook your food? No problem, RLP. We will do it just the way we did it for the Memorial Day cookout. We will break out our propane grill and cook outside! In a real life situation with no grid outage, a friend of mind fired up his grill for a cookout. Unfortunately, he did not consider the consequences of the grill heat on the vinyl siding right next to the grill on the patio. Vinyl siding melts and then catches on fire. If we are not thinking about fire prevention in an everyday situation, we may not be paying it the right amount of attention when we are cold, hungry, wet, or threatened.

Think about where you are most likely going to have the risks of a fire. Your kitchen, your garage, and your utility or laundry room are all good candidates. You will want to first prevent fires in those locations and then figure out how to fight fires in those locations. It is much better to keep your dryer exhaust from catching on fire in-the-first-place than trying to activate a fire extinguisher after-the-fact and then trying to subdue the flames inside of your wall.

Safety and Evacuation Plan

A safety and evacuation plan is not just for a business or commercial situation. Every home should have a written safety and evacuation plan, even if you have children that cannot read. A written plan helps you think through the process and brings clarity to your ideas. You will want to have some practice drills with your family but what kind of plan do you have in the case where you are hosting guests?

Emergency Procedures and Information Plan

Since it is so critical, RLP elected to include a sample [A009] Emergency Procedures and Information plan in a separate chapter plus a downloadable template for your use. This is not compromising operating security for the RLP family since it is only a sample plan and may or may not apply at all to the RLP family. However, it does point you in the right direction and lists types of risks and hazardous materials you may be dealing with in your own home.

Practice Drills

When the RLP family was younger, RLP would run practice drills in the middle of the night. This was a practical application and test of the Evacuation Plan. The family was expected to be able to exit their location and meet up safely even if they could not see. Sometimes RLP would even block the normal exit to make sure everyone could keep safe. No flashlights were allowed and certainly no candles were allowed.

Each drill was a learning experience. Did you know that a two-year old has difficulty operating a deadbolt on an exterior door? Did you know that the key has to be accessible to everyone in the home when the inside part of the lock is also keyed? Did you know that the garage door is more difficult to operate if there is no electricity?

RLP highly recommends that each family develop their own evacuation plan, develop their own practice drills, and then run their own drills. Every situation will be different. Fighting fires is the cool part. Your priorities should be: (1) preventing fires, (2) getting safe, (3) fighting fires. Part of getting safe is detecting fires. Many homes have house current only powered smoke or flame detectors. Others have battery backup systems but do not periodically test the batteries or detectors. Think about running the practice drills and testing your alarms at the same time. In a real life situation, are your children going to be woken up by you shaking their arm or the sound of the smoke detector?

Speaking of smoke detectors, RLP is sure that you have been repeatedly cautioned about periodically replacing the smoke detector batteries. This is not enough. Prevent the fire; do not just react to it when it occurs.

Fire Extinguishers

There have been entire books written about different classes of fires and different types of fire extinguishers. This is not one of those books. After inspecting many homes, RLP has discovered that a lot of homes do have the right type of fire extinguishers. However, the homeowners do not know where they are, do not have easy access to them, or do not know how to operate them. Fire extinguishers do little good in the original box stored somewhere in the basement. It is even worse if the fire extinguisher lost its charge last year.

After living on a Navy ship for years, RLP Is used to exposed pipes, accessible equipment, and color-coded everything. Not so much for MrsRLP. For some reason, she prefers the esthetically pleasing look. Each individual family is going to have to balance fire protection and safety with the requirements of good decorating taste.

After the top priority of preventing fires, the second priority is getting safe. It may make sense that you have your fire extinguisher in a location that supports that second priority. RLP recommends that you have your fire extinguisher accessible on the route out of the danger area. For instance, RLP has an appropriate fire extinguisher mounted just next to the people door exiting the garage to the outside.

Right next to that fire extinguisher is a device you may not have heard of but can be highly useful. Not surprisingly, it is painted red. Remember that you can extinguish a fire by removing the fuel? Natural gas is the fuel in a natural gas fire in your home. It would be convenient if you could shut off the natural gas or water supply to your house without having to wait for the fire department or utility company. You need to know how to do that by yourself and you have to have the right tool. RLP highly recommends your purchase something like the On Duty 4 in 1 Emergency Tool [L065] http://www.onduty1.com/ available at Amazon and other places. Make sure you test it for your situation. This combination tool can also be used to shut off the water main supplying your home.

Fire Place Fires

Chimney fires can be very dangerous. As usual, take steps to prevent them in the first place. But there are ways to help extinguish them when and if they occur. Please always first call for assistance if you have a chimney fire, even if you are absolutely confident that you can handle it. The *Real Life Prepper* is prepared for a chimney fire without having to retrieve the fire extinguisher and jam it into the wood burning stove or fireplace and then up the chimney. One of those preparations can be to invest into some fire suppressant sticks. Chimfex [L133] http://www.chimfex.us/ manufactures a stick that you treat like a flare. After activation, you simply toss the stick into the stove or fireplace and it uses zinc oxide fumes to extinguish the fire. These types of chimney fire extinguishers are very highly recommended. After your home is saved, please drop RLP a line to thank him.

Fire Protection Blankets

Another way to extinguish fires, particularly oil (kitchen) fires or people on fire is through the use of a fire blanket. RLP elected to include a link to Amazon rather than some of the regular fire blanket sites because sometimes they have axes to grind. A good selection is available at [L066] http://www.amazon.com/s?ie=UTF8&page=1&rh=i%3Aaps%2Ck%3AFire%20Blanket. You should research capabilities and search for a blanket on your own.

Structure Fires

I love policemen and firemen. They do great work. But sometimes they can get overwhelmed and overtaxed. If every home in your neighborhood is on fire, what kind of priority does your individual home have? Just recently, the only two access roads to our neighborhood were blocked totally. Some of the blockage was due to wrecked emergency vehicles. Virtually every emergency vehicle and all emergency personnel were occupied with an emergency somewhere. Even if emergency responders had prioritized my imaginary, scenario-generated house fire, they would not have been physically able to respond. This could have been a real life emergency. A structure fire without proper support is currently one of my most dreaded emergencies.

Yes, I could have broken out my lawn hoses and tried to put out the fire on my roof. I might have even asked my neighbor to lend assistance. A few regular lawn hoses do little to put out a burning house. And there is always the possibility that water pressure is not available, particularly in an emergency situation. In 1978, while in the Navy, I helped lead a team to fight a fire at sea on the Indian freighter, Jagat Padmini. There was no power on the freighter and no water pressure. We were forced to supply our own power and our own pressure. Fortunately, God supplied the water in the form of the Mediterranean Sea. Do you have a fire/water pump available? Is your house surrounded by the Mediterranean Sea? Mine is not.

There are alternatives, of course. Remember, your first priority is prevention! One alternative RLP has thought about is the backpack firefighting equipment available to civilians. This has not been proven by RLP, but is provided to give you ideas [L067] http://www.forestry-suppliers.com/product_pages/View_Catalog_Page.asp?mi=1579, particularly if you have woodlands around your house. If you can keep the leaves, grass, bushes, and trees around your house from burning, you may be able to keep your house from catching fire. This is probably not a good idea for fighting an actual home structure fire.

Water and Trash Pump

Even if you have a source of water, you must get it to the structure in order to make it useful. In an emergency situation, electricity may not be available. This means that you probably need a gasoline powered pump and sufficient hoses to deliver the water to the structure. Think about the consequences of using your pond on the other end of your suburban lot and sucking up a plastic bag into your pump. Pumps that are designed to operate successfully in that type of situation are sometimes known as trash pumps.

You can search for trash pumps on the internet as they are available everywhere. Northern Tool [L068] http://www.northerntool.com/shop/tools/category_water-pumps+engine-driven-pumps+engine-driven-full-trash-pumps has a good selection. Remember that you still need hoses and you need to prove that everything works. This kind of investment may suggest community or neighborhood cooperation.

Alternative Document Storage

In today's world, the computer is ubiquitous. But papers and photographs have not disappeared. Sometimes RLP believes that computers and printers have allowed us to generate even more paper than before.

When RLP was not at home one afternoon, MrsRLP was operating the washing machine in a rental home basement. The RLP family children were napping and the RLP family dog was just being a dog. The washing machine caught on fire. MrsRLP had evidently already thought through priorities as she rescued the children, rescued the dog, called for the fire department, and then reentered the building to rescue wedding pictures. RLP does want to save the wedding pictures and other documents but would much rather keep MrsRLP safe. In the real life world, we can take steps to reduce or even eliminate the risks and consequences of a structure fire damaging our precious pictures and documents without risking our more precious loved ones.

One of the solutions is to digitize all of the documents and store them in a place where they will be untouched by a home structure fire. This, of course, cannot protect your originals but the RLP family does not have that many Monet's hanging on the wall anyway. Photographs can be digitized and lose nothing in quality. In fact, it prevents normal degradation that normally occurs due to environmental factors.

As suggested earlier, you can make hard copies of documents, including placing them digitally on an extra external hard drive or USB drive and store them at an alternative location. RLP does not recommend a safety deposit box but rather recommends a relative or close friend. Even if you have a trusted family member or close friend available, your USB drive can still be stolen or misplaced. RLP highly recommends an encrypted USB drive such as the Patriot Bolt [L069] http://www.patriotmemory.com/product/detail.jsp?prodli ne=7&catid=86&prodgroupid=171&id=937&type=11,

Cruzer Glide [L070]
http://www.sandisk.com/products/usb/drives/cruzer-glide/ or my favorite, the IronKey [L035]
http://www.ironkey.com/en-US/encrypted-storage-drives/250-personal.html.

Another possible solution is to store your documents in a fire-proof safe such as a Liberty Safe [L040] http://www.libertysafe.com/ or Sentry Safe [L073] http://www.sentrysafe.com/. RLP does not recommend a safe with an electronic digital lock for this purpose. Can it be overkill to put your precious documents in a Sentry safe that is inside a Liberty safe? RLP says, "No, it is not overkill."

Keeping the USB drives up-to-date might become a hassle. There are other ways to backup your documents automatically. As long as you are connected to the internet, select documents can be automatically backed up to secure cloud storage. Documents can be restored anywhere. Rush Limbaugh used to (he may still) recommend Carbonite [L032] http://www.carbonite.com/. RLP offers no discount on, nor does he have any insight into Carbonite. RLP has personal experience with and recommends Mozy [L031] https://mozy.com. However, still no Mozy discount offer from RLP.

HYGIENE AND SANITATION

You Stink

Yes, you stink. So what is the big deal? Why might you want to not stink? You might offend your spouse and children. You might offend your co-workers. You might even offend yourself. But let's put this into the context of a survival situation. If you hunt, the animals will be able to detect you well before you detect them. If someone is hunting you and you are trying to hide, you can be detected a lot easier if you stink. This applies whether you are outside in the woods or in a building. Whether you know it or not, you can sometimes be detected through a closed door.

A few years ago, National Geographic magazine did a study about the sense of smell. Part of it was a survey where they put a scratch-and-sniff insert in the magazine and asked you to respond to questions. Would you eat this, wear this, or take a shower if it got on you? This world-wide survey revealed some interesting information. One of the most interesting things was that Americans stink, primarily because of the dairy and meat intake. But they do not really stink to other Americans. Let's get real here. Have you ever been to Europe?

It might be useful if we had a discussion about what stinks, how it stinks, and how you can keep it from stinking. There is a difference between fixing the stinking and covering up the offensive odor with another offensive or telltale odor. I am not sure what is worse in a tight elevator. Someone who just polished off a bag of Fritos? Someone who worked out in the gym yesterday and failed to shower? Or someone who splashed two ounces of aftershave over their neck and face?

Perfume stinks. Aftershave stinks. Hairspray

stinks. The solution to them is to not use them. Let's talk about general stinkiness of a different nature. What is it that stinks? Your breath, your skin, your perspiration, your hair, your feet, your arm pits, your clothes, your poop, and your pee all stink. Wow! How do we address this type of stinkiness? It is probably best handled on more than one level. Let's talk about cause, prevention, mitigation, and possibly even masking.

General Stinkiness

In case you were wondering, I made up the word "stinkiness." Much of our stinkiness comes from the inside. And no, this is not a theological discussion about our hearts. It is a physiological discussion about what makes you stink. Fundamentally, we stink from the inside. Our breath is highly impacted by what is going on with our entire digestive system, not just with the cleanliness of our mouth. Our perspiration is impacted by our health and what we have eaten. Think about when you have eaten garlic and then worked out. Think about when you have eaten asparagus and then urinated.

I think we can attack some of this stinkiness from the inside rather than trying to take care of it on the outside with mouthwash and underarm deodorant. At least part of this has already been addressed. Unfortunately, some folks have issues with their lower digestive track and must wear a colostomy bag. It might be embarrassing if the odor from the bag got to the wrong place at the wrong time. Somebody invented an internal deodorant to help mitigate this issue. There is no reason that someone else might not want to take advantage of the same solution without having the same problem. I did some research on this after reading an article in a hunting magazine. I tried two different products and decided that Nullo worked the best for me. Nullo is a chlorophyll-based tablet that acts very much like an internal deodorant. It does, in fact, work. My poop does not stink as much. Really. Granted, it is not perfect, but it is considerably better during hunting season than during the rest of the year. The Nullo website uses a byline, "Discover a way to neutralize body odor." It does not really neutralize body odor. But it does reduce odors from your breath, your arm pits, your urine, your feces, and even your feet.

Toilet Paper

Toilet paper is going to be worth its weight in gold. Think not? Try going even one day without it. You can never have too much for your own use and it would make a great barter item.

I am a hunter. My buddies and I spend a lot of time in the woods and sometimes nature calls unexpectedly. It is hard enough to take care of business when you have multiple layers of clothes on, a high-powered rifle over your shoulder, calf-high rubber boots on your feet, and a pack on your back while you are trying to keep quiet and scent free. Alas, the pack is the key. In it, every experienced hunter carries a flattened out, half-roll of toilet paper. So here is the story that started me on my quest.... My buddy had the irresistible urge while on foot, alone, in the north 40. The woods were wet from a recent rain but nature must be answered. Off came the rifle, pack, and coveralls. The hat stayed on. And yes! The baggie with the half-roll of toilet paper was in the pack. Gently, carefully, it was removed from the plastic bag and then just as carefully, dropped into the puddle left over from the rain. The entire roll became instantly unusable. My buddy quickly found a second use for his undershirt and socks.

There must be a better way. What if we could have reusable, water-resistant toilet paper? We can! Diaper services are still in operation around the country. The soiled cloth diapers are picked up by the diaper service, washed and sanitized, then reissued to the next family. But mothers are picky. They do not want to use frayed diapers or those that have very minor stains that cannot wash out. These used, soft, Grade B diapers are sold in bulk as rags. I thought we could buy some of these diapers, cut them in quarters, and stitch a hem around the cut edges. These quarter- diapers could easily be used as toilet paper, washed, and then be used again. Even if my buddy dropped one into the puddle, it is still usable whether wet or dry. In a grid-down situation, they could be kept in a diaper pail or bucket until they could be washed. It reminds me of many mission trips to Ecuador where the plumbing system could not handle toilet paper. The used paper had to go into an adjacent bucket with a lid for later disposal. Not much different. The used toilet paper went into the trash for future disposal whereas the diapers are washed like diapers and are reused.

Our research revealed a company in Lebanon, TN called "Smile Mommy Diaper Service". They had Grade B diapers they were planning on selling as rags. They were just as willing to sell me the rags and ship them to central AL. They were really inexpensive. Better yet, they also had cloth baby wipes exactly the same size as a quarter-diaper. I did not even know diaper services' supplied them. But they worked out even better as there was no cutting and no stitching required. They are perfect for carrying in my hunting pack. My food vacuum sealer packages a few cloth baby wipes as well as keeps them clean and dry. And they are perfect for when the schumer (literally) hits the fan.

Try it, you will thank me later.

Trash - Burn barrel
Have you ever wondered what you would do with your trash when and if the schumer hits?

Many folks have used a 55-gallon drum burn barrel or have one "just-in-case". This is probably not the best solution. It rusts out, is hard to start, does not burn hot, makes smoke, and does not burn everything as well as it should. Smoke attracts attention and really means everything is not burning as it should. Perhaps you should bury your trash? A couple of warnings here. In some states, it is illegal to burn your trash or use a burn barrel. In some states, you need a permit for a burn barrel or open pit fire but not for a fire behind a mesh screen. Which is where I am headed. If you burn certain materials, like plastic, they are likely to give off toxic gases. Bury that stuff.

After considerable research, I found two good sources of stainless steel burn cages. They are expensive, but probably worth it. The first is made by DR.Power. If you go to [L044] http://www.DRpower.com/AMG you might get a $70 discount (NRA sponsored). It is square and used to be US made. It is now made in China. Visit the website and learn even if you have not decided to buy one. The other choice is a round (probably stronger) cage made by Burn Right Products [L045] (burnrightproducts.com). They might have a $55 off fall sale and they have a military discount. Do not know if you can use both discounts at the same time. We could not tell for sure if they are US made. These stainless steel burn cages are designed to burn at about 1,600 degrees and give off very little smoke. The covers (round covers are more structurally sound – less tendency to warp - than square covers) minimize the threat of spreading a fire accidentally. The DR.Power square burn barrels fold flat in theory. The round ones do not and thus are harder to store. They both seem to be environmentally sound. I am going for the Burn Right.

Trash Bags

Like toilet paper, you can never have enough trash bags. And like most good prepper items, they have more than one use. Leaving trash around is not good operational security and is just not being a good citizen. Besides being able to track you, folks can tell what you are throwing away: ammo boxes, MRE residue, dehydrated meal packages, etc. Once when RLP and MrsRLP were in Italy (Venice) on a vacation, we were starving. I am not a real fan of real Italian food. Fortunately, there were some open top trash cans around. Always observant of my surroundings, I spotted the telltale Big Mac wrapper in the top of the trash bin from across the court yard. We were saved! It was just an academic exercise to track the wrappers back to the queen bee where we feasted on Big Macs and hot fires. It would be a lot easier for me to track you to your campsite.

Every good hunter keeps a roll of plastic trash bags in his or her pack. A trash bag can completely contain the pack that is not normally waterproof. Another can also completely cover the expensive hunting rifle that you do not want to get wet. Imagine gutting a deer to make it lighter to carry out of the woods. Now your carefully laundered hunting clothes are bloody, smell like deer guts, and are probably wet with perspiration. You reach into your pack, pull out your clean hunting clothes from the plastic trash bag and put your messed up clothes in a waterproof, contained trash bag. Most rolls of plastic trash bags that we are talking about are actually rolls placed in a cardboard box for marketing. You do not need to carry that box around with you.

Other times you may want to use a paper trash bag. Think about it when you are at the grocery store and they ask you, "Paper or plastic?" If you shred your confidential personal information, you may want to put the shred residue in a paper bag and toss it, bag and all, in your burn barrel. Much cleaner than a plastic bag.

Then again, sometimes plastic is better. Some ingenious folks designed and sell a toilet seat that fits on the top of a five-gallon plastic bucket. This can come in very handy when needed. Rather than cleaning out the five-gallon bucket, you may want to line it first with a trash bag. Would you rather use a plastic or a paper trash bag? A scoop of lime in the plastic bag can go a long way towards keeping things pleasant. You can always bury the sealed plastic bag if needed.

RLP also makes good use of what we call Walmart bags. They are the cheap, smaller plastic bags you get from Walmart. Did I mention they are free? They take up little room, are disposable, and are handy for many things. MrsRLP keeps a bag of bags in the basement and we rely on them frequently.

Sewage
When we were first married and looking for a house, there was at least one thing that was a litmus test for the house. Our purchase had the requirement that we were hooked up to the city or county sewer system. But that was when were younger and did not know any better. The government will take care of us! Now that we are wiser, we still have a litmus test. We must be hooked up to our own septic tank. The environmental impact of a municipal sewage treatment plant, other than for highly dense city (something that must be avoided anyway) is phenomenally bad. And the government will not take care of us. Think Jefferson County, Alabama or my parents' modest home in Florida where they pay more for sewage than they do for water.

The unfortunate thing about the current design of septic systems is that we do not properly account for nor do we properly manage grey water and black water. There is no reason we should pump my shower water or our laundry water into the same settling tank where my dinner eventually goes. If you have the opportunity, RLP highly recommends [L046] *The New Create an Oasis with Greywater: Choosing, Building and Using Greywater Systems - Includes Branched Drains.* It is available from Amazon.

Regardless, if properly managed, your own private septic system will last longer than a municipal sewage treatment plant.

Porta-potty

There are things out there beyond outhouses. RLP has the only trailer/camper at the hunting camp with no sewage connection. And there is no outhouse available. Trees work for some things but for other things, you just need to sit down. An alternative is a porta-potty. RLP highly recommends [L047] the Thetford 92360 Porta Potti 550E Curve Portable Toilet. Yes, it uses batteries. But it pumps a little water from a holding tank through the business container and into a holding tank. It uses the same blue stuff to keep things sanitary that an RV uses. And it is comfortable. MrsRLP will appreciate it more than sitting over a wet log in the middle of the woods. The holding tank detaches and can be dumped into a regular toilet. This type of facility is a temporary convenience used primarily in a marine environment. A longer term solution may be a dry compost toilet.

Dry Compost Toilet

Like most things, there are different opinions about using human compost for "compost". If it is your family and you know what diseases and parasites you have, I see no problem with it. Ever lived in Germany? Honey wagons distribute unprocessed or slightly processed human sewage (from people you do not know) to farmers' fields on a daily basis. You can still dry compost and put the nutrients on the hedges protecting the borders to your property.

The whole process is not as clean as Americans would like it to be, but it is a doable thing. This works particularly well if you are in a marine environment such as a sail boat. If you are not on a restricted space sail boat, it can even work better. The best dry compost toilet I have seen is in fact, dry. The proper equipment diverts urine to a separate collection tank so that the other stuff can be processed dry. The other stuff can be used on your plants. Your mileage may vary, but it can be used on the plants you eat, particularly trees. A dry compost toilet works without batteries and without water. As far as I can tell, it works without any significant smell.

RLP recommends the [L048] C-Head or BoonJon Portable Composting Toilet Systems. This is one of those things where you will be thanking RLP years down the road. You are welcome. You owe it to yourself and to your family to at least consider this and learn from the information on the site.

Baby Wipes

Baby wipes are not just for baby's butts! This is another thing I learned at my hunting camp with no running water. I want my hands clean after taking care of business of one type or another but I do not want them to smell like a baby's bottom. I discovered unscented baby wipes. They are alcohol free, moist enough, and strong enough to wash my face, or my hands, or my pits. And they do not smell! Since they come in a sealed plastic box, they have a very long shelf life. If you reseal them, they keep fresh and moist for a long time. Even Walmart sells a plastic dispenser box with a refill pack and a travel pack. Highly recommended for general use although I would not use them to sterilize a table just before I removed somebody's appendix with my pocket knife by the light of a candle.

Flushing Water

Let's assume you do not have a bidet. (They are fabulous by the way.) You then need no electricity to flush your toilet. You just need water. Gravity and water take care of all the action that needs to take place to make you feel like you are still connected with civilization. As long as you are on your septic system, there is nothing to prevent your plumbing from working like it is designed to do. If your municipal sewage system blocks up, you are in trouble. Stuff runs down hill and chances are you are downhill from at least one of your neighbors. I know of more than one person who found out that their basement toilet was the low point in their household plumbing. Generally either there is no check valve between your household sewage system and the street sewer line or it does not work as designed.

If the water supply to your house fails, you might be in trouble. Besides no drinking water, how are you going to flush your toilet? First, remember that the water in your toilet tank (not bowl) may be potable or can be easily cleaned for drinking water. Also remember that the water in your tank that flushes waste into your sewage system does not have to be potable. You do not want to kill the good bacteria in your septic system but it does not have to be pristine. Seawater is not recommended. You can use water directly from your pond or lake. And remember to take out the big chunks and fish before you store it in a plastic bucket next to your regular toilet. Refilling the tank makes things a little more civilized but pouring the water directly into the bowl works too. This works both for your own septic system and for your municipal sewage system. Another great source is your downspout collector barrels gathering water from your roof. This water does not have to be processed before use in your tank.

Shovel

A shovel, along with an axe, may be the ultimate survival tool. If you do not yet have a shovel, please gather all of the survival books you have already purchased and return them. You will not need them.

People poop is nasty. It contains diseases, human parasites, and it stinks. And animals like it. They will find it and eat it or at least rub themselves in it and distribute it anywhere they can. What this means is that if you poop in a trench and do not adequately cover it, some animal will find it. In fact, an animal otherwise known as a bad guy may also find it. Remember, you stink. You need a good shovel to bury it where animals cannot get to it. You also need to protect your water supply. Do not bury the poop upstream or uphill of any water supply. This includes placement of your outhouse. Current thumb rules suggest a 3-5 foot hole placed 20-100 feet downstream of(or away from) a water source. Try doing that without having a shovel!

In an emergency situation, just use the shovel to dig yourself a hole first and then cover up/bury your waste. A small camp shovel is handier than your hands for this purpose.

CLOTHING AND LAUNDRY

Neither regular clothing nor laundry really held an interest for RLP. However, RLP never wanted MrsRLP to take care of his hunting clothes. Scent control was always an issue. As an NRA instructor, many folks also asked questions about the proper gear to wear to manage concealed carry gear. Still, RLP was always concerned about what would happen if the laundry could not be done in the typical suburbanite fashion with a washing machine and dryer.

Washing Clothes

Many folks might think we are leaving the world of *Real Life Prepper* and entering the world of *Doomsday Prepper* when discussing washing clothes in other than a regular home type washing machine. However, RLP believes it should be at least addressed for completeness. Remember, this is a journey, not a destination.

RLP highly recommends that you invest a little thought into the process even if you do not make any other preparations. Lehman's [L119] https://www.lehmans.com/default.aspx offers a number of alternatives including galvanized washtubs, agitators, and hand washers. Their website is an interesting read and knowledge is weightless. I guess that MrsRLP would prefer this type of solution before we settled on the big rock in the backyard creek.

Drying Clothes

The *Real Life Prepper* normally uses an electric or a natural gas dryer to dry the family clothes. RLP's mother always had access to an outdoor clothes line. Those outdoor clotheslines have now fallen into disfavor with neighborhood and homeowner associations. But what are you going to do if there is a grid outage lasting more than just a few days? RLP highly recommends you invest in some regular clothespins and some simple clothes lines (rope). Even if the homeowner association objects to an outside line, you might still be able to set up a line in your garage or basement. This is not a skill that has to be proven and practiced. Buy the materials and keep them in the original packages until needed.

Whitmor [L117] http://whitmor.com/index.php manufactures an inexpensive, folding, epoxy coated drying rack that does not even require clothespins or clothesline. Taking up little storage room with easy setup and takedown, the drying rack is a good investment.

Scent Control and UV

White tail deer see very well in the ultraviolet (UV) region of the light spectrum. RLP did a considerable amount of research before settling on a good solution that managed both UV and scent control. RLP is highly impressed with the Atsko [L118] http://www.atsko.com/ line of UV and scent control products. Black light and UV flashlights are good devices that can be used to prove the effectiveness of the wash yourself.

Make Your Own Laundry Soap

Now we are really starting to sound like *Doomsday Preppers*! However, RLP has a family friend that makes her own laundry soap because she prefers it and she believes it to be cheaper than commercial laundry detergent. Lehman's [L119] https://www.lehmans.com/default.aspx sells virtually all of the supplies you need to make your own laundry soap. You can also purchase most or all of the materials locally. This family friend is already well on her way to being prepared in case the zombie apocalypse interrupts the supply of laundry detergent to her large family.

Laundry Soap Recipe

- One 4-pound, 12 ounce box Borax (2.15 kg or 76 ounce) found in the detergent aisle
- One 4-pound Arm & Hammer Baking Soda (1.81 kg) found in the cooking aisle
- One 55-ounce box Arm & Hammer Super Washing Soda (3 pound, 7 ounce) found in the detergent aisle
- Three bars of Fels-Naptha soap found in the detergent aisle. If you use Zote bars instead, only use two bars. Zote is available at Home Depot.
- Optional – two small containers of Oxy Clean or store brand Oxy Clean. Try to get around 3.5 pounds (1.58 kg) found in the detergent aisle.
- The detergent is fairly mild smelling and not overpowering. If you want a strong scent, you can add some fabric softener or laundry crystals to each load. Laundry crystal can be found in the detergent aisle.
- Start out by grating the Fels-Naptha soap just like cheese. You can use a food processor or just use your handheld grater. Those of you with a high efficiency (HE) washer may want to run the mix through the grater again to get an even finer mix. The Fels-Naptha will dissolve even in the cold. Mix all ingredients together in a large lined, five-gallon plastic bucket. It does not have to be a food grade bucket. Stir well. You might want to close the bag and shake it to aid in the mixing.

Holsters

When RLP first began investigating carrying a firearm, he made inquiries into holsters and received the same warning from many sources. Everyone advised him that when complete, he would end up with a box full of different holsters. Every source was incorrect. RLP ended up with two boxes of holsters.

Among other things, holsters can be categorized by:

- Material of construction
- Attachment mechanism
- Attachment location
- Retention method

Holster Material

RLP first started out purchasing a holster manufactured from cheap, stitched nylon. It was comfortable, soft, and flexible but did not offer the level of security desired. RLP Is embarrassed to reveal that on its own volition, his firearm elected to leap from that holster onto a friend's living room floor one evening when RLP shifted suddenly on the couch. That holster now remains unused in the box. The friend remains wary and unimpressed.

Although highly recommended by law enforcement friends, RLP never made the foray into leather holsters. RLP was much more interested in functionality than in appearance, particularly since the holster would almost always be carrying a concealed firearm. Even when carrying open, like when on the range, a Kydex (think plastic) holster seemed to make more sense because of the perceived durability. And RLP highly recommends consistency when practicing life skills that can in fact, save your life.

Holster Attachment Mechanism

Because of the nature of our society, RLP does not always carry a firearm. That means the holster itself should be able to be easily attached and detached. For that purpose, most folks start out with a clip or a paddle holster attachment. RLP highly recommends that the regular clip attachment not be seriously considered on a routine basis. However, in certain circumstances and configurations, a clip may be your best bet.

The foundational attachment device, such as the paddle, is not necessarily restrictive as to the holster mechanism itself. RLP wore a paddle holster for a number of years before discovering that the holster could be mounted on a variety of foundational platforms. The paddle, usually made of Kydex, reminds me of the business end of a small ping-pong paddle. The holster itself is secured to the paddle by screws. The flat or barely curved paddle slips in between the belt and the pants or between the pants and belt combination and the skin effectively securing the holster to the body. (The paddle can be slipped inside the pants without a belt but it is not very secure.) The paddle, and thus the holster, can be attached and detached from the body without having to remove the belt.

For RLP, the more preferred attachment mechanism is belt loops. Rather than using a paddle, the foundation is two Kydex belt loops and the holster mechanism is secured to the foundation by the same screws used when securing it to the paddle. In order to attach or detach the holster, the belt must be removed and reinserted into the belt loops of the pants as well as the holster foundation.

Holster Attachment Location

The two primary choices here are Inside the Waistband (IWB) and Outside the Waistband (OWB). An IWB holster foundation, holster, and firearm all ride primarily inside your pants. An OWB holster foundation, holster, and firearm all ride primarily outside of your pants. If you wear a 32-inch waist size pants and attempt to put in a two or three inch holster and pistol combination inside your pants, you may have some difficulties.

After deciding IWB or OWB, the next choice is, "Where on my waist do I put it?" RLP recommends you experiment. But once you complete your experiments, strive for consistently and practice what you will do every day.

Folks who shoot use terms such as strong hand and weak hand. Your strong hand is the arm or hand you use to actually operate the firearm on a normal basis. Most folks are right-handed and their strong hand is their right side. Most folks wear their firearm holster on their strong side and if they carry a magazine holster, wear that on the weak side. The weak hand is normally used to manage your magazines and reload.

Whether using an IWB or OWB holster, most folks end up carrying them in one of two primary positions: appendix carry or hip carry. They both have advantages and disadvantages. Considering your navel as North or 0 degrees, appendix carry is about 45 degrees. 90 degrees is straight out of your side. Hip carry is slightly more than 90 degrees, but perhaps not as much as 135 degrees. Imagine if you are carrying a concealed firearm in the appendix carry position and a breeze opens up your covering. You may not want to have to answer questions raised by the sudden appearance of this valuable tool of American freedom. For the *Real Life Prepper* with either strong side, the butt of the firearm will be facing towards your backbone with your thumb in between your firearm and your body. RLP recommends either the hip carry position or straight out of your strong side (90 degrees).

An alternative carry position is in the small of your back. At first blush, this seems to make a lot of sense. It is very easy to conceal and can be comfortable when walking or even driving in the car. Consider the implications of falling down on the flat of your back. You will probably not appreciate the impact. In addition, your strong hand will have to be reversed as your firearm butt will be pointing in the opposite direction. Your firearm will be in between your thumb and your body.

Firearm Retention Method

Many times, friction can be your friend. Friction can easily provide all of the retention you need. Many holsters have adjustment screws so you can adjust the amount of tension or friction you need for security and comfort.

Other folks seem to worry about their firearm being taken from their holster by someone else. Law enforcement officers (LEOs) are particularly worried about this circumstance. Retention degree is described in levels. Sometimes passive retention is described by Level 0, or no retention other than friction.

- Level 0 – Passive or friction only retention.
- Level 1 – A single retention device such as a thumb break.
- Level 2 – Combines a level 1 feature with an additional active safety measure such as pressing a button. The Blackhawk Serpa [L123] http://www.blackhawk.com/catalog/Holsters,16. htm appears to be the most popular civilian Level 2 holster.
- Level 3 – Incorporates three active security devices. Level 3 is used almost exclusively in the LEO community.

Although the Blackhawk Serpa appears to be a very popular holster, it is banned in certain training venues, including Front Sight. The Serpa is very intuitive but requires you to press a button with your trigger finger to free up the retention as you withdraw the firearm from the holster. In a state of excitement, one may continue to press with the trigger finger and it can end up in the trigger guard, subsequently activating the trigger which might result in shooting yourself in the leg.

CrossBreed Holsters [L130]
http://www.crossbreedholsters.com/ markets a great line
of IWB and OWB holsters. RLP recommends you
investigate the horsehide leather rather than the cow
leather if you decide to go with a CrossBreed IWB
holster. They are highly recommended.

Blade-Tech Holster Review

RLP used to normally carry concealed using a
Blackhawk Serpa. The Serpa is banned at Front Sight so
I needed a new holster for training. The Blade-Tech
holster [L124] http://shop.blade-tech.com/index.php was
cheap enough to use for a four-day class so I got one for
a G17 and one for a G23. Both guns fit the same and feel
the same. There is no sense that the Glock(s) would fall
out of the holster (a great fear of mine), even when
running. The holster is designed to go on belt loops -
BUY A GUN BELT - and can be a little awkward when
positioning. I put the belt through the back holster loop,
a pants loop, then the forward holster loop. It makes it
much more secure but limits the travel around the
circumference of your waist. It can only go back and
forth until the holster loop meets the pants loop. A belt
loop holster is not as convenient as a paddle holster.
However, the holster conforms well to the curvature of
my body and lies pretty flat making it much easier to
conceal. The Kydex/plastic at the top between my body
and the gun was uncomfortable at first and sort of stuck
in my ribs when I twisted or sat down wrong. After a
while (when I became used to it), the sensation became
unnoticeable. It is designed to protect your skin and the
firearm from sweat. I never adjusted the tensioning
screw and the tension did not appear to change. After
about 1,000 draws and re-insertions for each holster in
four days, there is just a barely detectable wear mark on
the holster (it may even rub off with my fingers) and

none on the gun. The only problem with the holster is based on the style - you have to take your belt off to mount or un-mount the holster. Perhaps I should have bought the Blade-Tech before the Serpa.

Gun Belt

Whereas the proper holster is the key element in safely and comfortably carrying a firearm, the gun belt is the secret element that can give you the most confidence and greatly enhance your security. Some self-appointed fashion expert decided that thinner belts are better looking but they sure do not work that well as a gun belt. They do not hold up to the weight of a firearm holster, firearm, magazine holster, and magazine. The thin belts collapse, sag, or flip over and everything feels like it is going to end up around your ankles. RLP decided that he needed to ignore good fashion sense and be prepared with a belt that would hold up if necessary. Unfortunately, the belt designers conspired with the pants designers and "slacks" only come with narrow belt loops to accommodate the thin belts.

A proper gun belt is substantial enough to withstand the weight and other forces placed on it by your gear. A proper gun belt is not a LEO duty belt. It is just bigger and beefier than a regular belt. Generally they are not decorative but they do not have to be ugly. A good gun belt is usually made of leather (sometimes very thick) and somewhere between one and ¼ inch and one and ½ inch tall. After you purchase a gun belt or two, you then face the search for the holy grail in trying to find pants with belt loops large enough to accommodate your gun belt. Even regular jeans sometimes do not have belt loops large enough to accommodate a proper gun belt.

RLP visited the Blade-Tech [L124] http://shop.blade-tech.com/index.php display booth at a trade show and purchased a prototype sample gun belt. It worked out great and is highly recommended.

RLP's waist size changes depending on what I had for supper and the type of pants I am wearing. Since most belts rely on hole spacing that is fixed, sometimes the belts are too tight and sometimes they are too loose.

An alternative to fixed hole spacing is Velcro that gives infinite adjustments. One of these types of belts is called a Wilderness Instructor Belt [L125] http://www.thewilderness.com/tactical-belts/. Although perhaps not as attractive as leather belt, they have a lot of great features including coming in at least three colors. Both RLP and MrsRLP highly recommend the instructor belt. The only issue with this belt is how one puts it on. Normally you feed the end of the belt into your left-hand pants belt loops with your right hand. After the tip reaches the belt buckle, it curls back through the buckle and affixes to itself using Velcro. The now double thickness belt may be too thick to accommodate the holster belt loops comfortably at the hip carry position. The problem is resolved by initially feeding the end of the belt into your right-hand pants belt loops (going clockwise instead of counter-clockwise).

Regular Holster Alternatives

"Hey, RLP! The 80s called and they want their fanny pack back!" In my case, it is better termed a "belly bag." Some folks believe that wearing a belly bag is a sure sign of carrying a concealed firearm. Others just think it is a sure sign of just getting old. However, sometimes you do what you have to do. RLP believes that carrying a firearm in a belly bag can be a viable alternative under the correct circumstances. The pack is usually directly in front of you with the firearm in a secure holster within the main compartment. The main compartment opens rapidly with one oversize zipper pull (usually using your weak hand) allowing you to properly grip and withdraw the firearm with one (the strong) hand. The fanny pack or belly bag is not allowed in some range venues because the loaded firearm is pointing at the person next to you as you are withdrawing it from the holster.

If you are visiting an establishment that indicates all purses, packs, and bags are subject to search, this includes your belly bag. They are not as likely to look under your shirt or vest or pat you down. If you want to conceal while wearing shorts and a T-shirt, a belly bag may just fit the bill. RLP is concerned about the possibility of being physically separated from the belly bag, similar to the situation where you may conceal your firearm in your purse and sit it down on the table.

Gun gear [L126] http://www.gungear.com/ez-catalog/X300536/3 has a good demonstration and guide to both concealed carry belly bags and concealed carry purses.

Concealed Comfort [L127] http://www.concealedcomfort.com/ markets a specialized holster that mimics the ubiquitous cell phone. RLP has no experience actually wearing this device although it looks intriguing.

For deep concealment, Belly Band Holster [L128] http://bellybandccw.com/ markets an elastic holster that fits totally under your shirt. Check out the Thunderwear holster while you are doing your research.

Vests
Vests are cool! RLP loves pockets and vests usually come with many pockets. Some of the folks that believe a belly bag is a sure sign that you are carrying a

concealed firearm also believe that a vest also points in the same direction. There are several types of vests and the tactical type vest may actually deserve that reputation. Photographer's vests do not necessarily share that image. RLP does not recommend you wear a vest with a holster built into one of the inside pockets. It causes the vest to drape abnormally and can get uncomfortable. RLP recommends you use the vest to cover your regular IWB or OWB holster at the hip carry position. Vests come in different lengths so make sure you try them carefully before you rely on them for good concealment. RLP is a particular fan of the Scott E Vest [L129] https://www.scottevest.com/ for lots of pockets and great concealment.

The search for the holy grail never really ends. RLP is always on the lookout for pants with adequately sized belt loops. MrsRLP is always on the lookout for pants that look good.

Tru Spec 24-7 Tactical Pants Review

I love these pants! I bought a single pair of the Tru-Specs [L131] http://www.truspec.com/ from the U.S. Cavalry store in Columbus, GA thinking I would have to shorten them by two inches. Not so, they fit perfectly two inches longer than my normal size. They are uber-comfortable and look more like slacks then cargo pants. I love the multiple pockets and they work much better in a tactical reload than regular jeans. The material is naturally stain repellant/resistant and needs no ironing. I received a different brand of high-end "tactical" pants for Christmas that cost over $100. They were returned and I bought three more pair of Tru-Specs. I also got some knee padding inserts for use when needed. The pants are available online in several places including Amazon. The dyeing is not consistent - not that it matters that much to me. This is not meant to imply an individual pair of pants is not consistently colored. It means that the khaki pants I bought in one place are a slight shade different than the khaki pants for sale in a different location. Who cares? I am not an operator. I just wear them to work. Even MrsRLP thinks they look good. Highly recommended!

COMPUTER PREPARATIONS

UPS

Even if the zombie apocalypse does not hit your house, a lightning bolt or power outage might. The single greatest thing you can do to physically protect your computer and data is to purchase and use an uninterruptible power supply (UPS). There used to be many manufacturers but American Power Conversion (APC) [L065] http://apc.com has the lion's share today. Essentially they are a pack of 12-volt gel type batteries that are constantly being charged by your street/house power. Although the batteries put out 12 volts DC, an electronic device changes that to 110/120 volts AC that your computer uses. Your computer constantly runs off that UPS AC power, not your house current. That way, the power is never interrupted (at least until the batteries run out of their stored charge). In addition, that AC power is conditioned, or much cleaner than your house current. In fact, if you have a brown out, rather than a black out, the batteries will even add enough power to maintain power at the minimum requirements. Nicer (read that as expensive) APC equipment comes with communication software and cables to automatically shut down your computer gracefully if the batteries get near to losing their charge. If you use Windows, like most of us do, you already know that an ungraceful shutdown is not pretty. UPS devices are available everywhere, including Amazon. You may get a better deal at Sam's or Costco.

Inverter Generator

Generators are a complex topic all by themselves. Most household generators change speed based on the load. This basically means that the frequency may change when the load changes. This is not good for fuel efficiency or for your computer that is expecting clean power. More expensive generators, usually made by companies such as Honda, Yamaha, and Champion, may be designed as inverter generators. They run at a constant speed and use an inverter to make clean AC power. In essence, they make a clean sine wave rather than a square wave. If you want to take the best step to protect your sensitive electronic equipment with a generator, spend the extra money and buy an inverter generator. As mentioned, they are more fuel efficient. They are also generally smaller and quieter. This makes them more ideal for camping trips. Most of these smaller capacity inverter generators can be run in parallel with an identical model (after you purchase the kit) to double the capacity.

Backups and Data Security

Chances are you have a computer and use email. You probably have some irreplaceable photographs on your computer. You may have some financial records and even access to your bank accounts on your computer. It is in your best interest that you provide some security for that data and access. Since entire books have been written to address these issues, we will only hit some highlights and perhaps give you some additional perspective.

Make no mistake about it. The government either already has access to your email or is trying to get it. The NSA claims they are just gathering metadata (data about data) but they, and marketers, are reading your email. Often we will mention a subject only in an email. The next time we use Google to search an unrelated topic, advertisements regarding the subject mentioned only in the email show up in the browser.

Even if the identity thieves and the government are not trying to get your data, a fire or tornado might. RLP has several different recommended strategies that you might employ to help you protect your data and then recover if you need to. The first strategy is the use of an online backup system. Although they charge for their services, they have two major advantages. First, once you get it setup, it is automatic. Second, you can restore from anywhere to anywhere. The two major services are: [L031] http://www.mozy.com/ and [L032] http://www.carbonite.com . The second strategy is the use of an automatic application that backs up to an extra, external hard drive hooked up to your computer using a USB connection. Western Digital [L033] http://www.wdc.com/en/ is one vendor who offers this type of solution. An advantage of the external hard drive is that you have control of it. A disadvantage of the external hard drive is that it is subject to theft or environmental damage in the same fashion as your computer since it is sitting right next to it.

A third solution is an encrypted thumb drive (USB flash drive). SanDisk [L034] http://www.sandisk.com offers a line of encrypted thumbs drives that are store up to 32GB for $18-$49. RLP recommends you look at the products available from IronKey [L035] http://www.ironkey.com . Remember *Mission Impossible*? The IronKey thumb drive will self-destruct if there are ten failed, consecutive password attempts. It is waterproof and expensive. The 32GB thumb drive can cost $100-$500.

Swapping thumb drives and other information is a proven strategy that enables data recovery. Find a like-minded buddy that does not live really close to you. Develop a plan to periodically swap data. Each of you can store a lock box in the other person's house. In the lock box, store multiple thumb drives and copies of irreplaceable documents such as birth, marriage, and death certificates.

RLP highly recommends you encrypt at least your email. There are several for profit, commercial companies providing disk and email encryption tools. I cannot guarantee that they have not sold themselves out to the government. Although the possibility of backdoor access is always present, it is less likely if the source code is open source. A commercial version of Pretty Good Privacy (PGP) is available from Symantec [L036] http://www.symantec.com/encryption . If you are computer savvy at all, we recommend you purchase and read *PGP & GPG: Email for the Practical Paranoid* by Michael W. Lucas. GPG is essentially the open source (and free) version of PGP.

If you are like RLP and do not trust Google or Microsoft (Bing), you may want to use another search engine in your browser. One alternative is Startpage [L037] https://startpage.com/. They say they are "the world's most private search engine." Another alternative is DuckDuckGo [L038] https://duckduckgo.com/ where they "Search anonymously. Find instantly."

If you are really, really concerned about your personal privacy, explore Tor [L039] https://www.torproject.org/ which, among other things, allows you to circumvent some of the surveillance that is going on. One of the best things available is the Tor on a thumb drive that allows you to surf the net from the thumb drive without even leaving a fingerprint on the PC it is plugged into.

Digital Privacy

Sovereign Man [L143] http://www.sovereignman.com/ is a good source for some digital privacy information. RLP has placed his Digital Privacy Black Paper [A006] on the companion website Reallifeprepper.com for your use and information.

COMMUNITY

In early 2014, Alabama was hit by a freak snow storm. RLP's office closed at 10:30 AM. An officemate was able to transport RLP just a few miles towards his neighborhood on his 17-mile trip. MrsRLP then picked up RLP and headed for home. At 1:00 AM the next morning, a hero (stranger) who happened by on his 4x4 ATV rescued RLP and transported him the rest of the way to his subdivision. This was not community but rather the kindness of a good man.

RLP believes that real community is one of the most important elements of being a *Real Life Prepper*. Community is also one of the hardest elements to build and maintain. Many folks believe that if you are alone when the schumer hits the fan, you are going to die. Although the freak storm was not the zombie apocalypse, in RLP's world, the schumer had hit the fan.

Because of the current state of our society, it is almost much easier to develop a false sense of community over the internet and not even know who your physical neighbors are. RLP is guilty of communicating many more times with someone 2,000 miles away than with someone two doors away. In the freak snowstorm, RLP's neighbor might have needed some assistance. The RLP family may have needed some assistance. Since we had not built community in advance, we were all unprepared.

Every reasonably sized neighborhood has its share of widows, invalids, and folks who just suffer from an accident. It could have been us. Most folks in the neighborhood did not check up on the RLP family. With no support structure, all of the preparations you have made can turn into a waste of time and just seem silly.

RLP is certainly not advocating a commune or a nest of busybodies. Even in the absence of the zombie apocalypse, real community makes sense. RLP may know how to do rough carpentry but a neighbor may know how to weld. Perhaps one of the most important lessons RLP has learned in life is that as much as he tries, he cannot know everything and do everything by himself. The big question is, "How do you build community?"

Build Trust

Real community cannot be easily built at 1:00 AM the morning after a freak snowstorm, although it can help. In a previous neighborhood, RLP reached out after a hurricane to help clear a neighbor's fallen tree. The day after the 2014 freak snowstorm, MrsRLP worked with a neighbor to help feed many hungry Mother's Day Out children and adults stuck in a local church. What both of these incidents did was to build trust and make an investment into the community bank. Small catastrophes can help break down barriers and help build trust. RLP believes that we need to be more intentional in building real community.

As mentioned in the Fire Protection chapter, a large water or trash pump with hoses may one day be useful in controlling a structure fire in your neighborhood. It may even be your house that is saved with the water from your neighbor's pond or pool. With trust (built in advance) and real community, there exists a better probability of true cooperation between neighbors.

Summer may be the best time to build real community in your neighborhood. Lend a hand and ask for help. Take a walk around the neighborhood and greet folks. Eat together. Have a neighborhood cookout.

Neighborhood Watch

Regardless of what you have read about the Zimmerman and Martin tragedy, a Neighborhood Watch program can still develop good connections in a neighborhood. It is not beyond your capability to start one from scratch if it does not already exist. There are plenty of resources on the internet to help you along. Most law enforcement agencies are still behind them and will support you.

Leverage Technology

There are many newer systems that allow you to build community in your neighborhood and even in the surrounding area. Everyone who reads *Real Life Prepper* will not live in a typical suburban subdivision but everyone still needs community. Meetup.com [L104] http://www.meetup.com/ is one such technology and typically reaches out to areas or zip codes rather than individual neighborhoods. Many groups establish initial contact, manage ongoing contacts, and arrange for meetings through Meetup.com. They do charge a fee for the organizer but it can easily be worth the investment.

Facebook can be both a curse and a blessing. Facebook allows you to establish a member-only, private group to share information. The RLP neighborhood just established a Facebook group to provide neighborhood information and seek assistance when necessary. If you believe that this is really secure, RLP has some swamp land in Florida that he would like to sell you.

Some ambitious or "called" prepper also has the option of developing and maintaining an internet forum or bulletin board to share requests and information. This type of forum has the possibility of appealing to a national audience and thus may not be the optimum path for someone strictly trying to establish local community.

IPS [L105] http://www.invisionpower.com/ provides the infrastructure for a great forum but just like Meetup.com, charges a maintenance fee to the organizer.

MIG versus MAG

RLP actively runs a Mutual Interest Group (MIG) but only participates in the community of a Mutual Assistance Group (MAG). The MIG meets monthly to share information and learn from each other. Recently we met to take a tour of a deer processing facility. The next month we met to discuss how to build one of those evil black things liberals love to hate. A MIG may participate in group learning situations and even leverage group buys. Currently, only RLP knows who is on the MIG list. Everyone else is totally anonymous except where individual connections are made at the monthly meetings. Trust is built in an organic and natural way.

A MAG may lean more toward a *Doomsday Prepper* than a *Real Life Prepper*. Many MAGs are planning on actively living and working together when the schumer hits the fan. Consider a MAG as having all of the benefits of a MIG but taking it to the next level.

MISCELLANEOUS ITEMS

Matches

Just because your nanny government does not want you to use real matches does not mean matches might come in handy sometime. There was a concerted effort a few years ago to totally ban kitchen matches (the kind that strike anywhere). RLP recommends you invest in some so called storm proof matches that come in their own waterproof case. Industrial Revolution makes some UCO storm proof matches [L134] http://industrialrev.com/stormproof-match-kit.html that burn better and longer than normal, even after being submerged in water. The plastic case keeps them secure and ready to go. Buy several kits and keep some in your GHB as well as in your kitchen.

Another alternative is to vacuum pack a box of kitchen matches to store in your GHB. They will keep safe, dry, and organized.

Mercy and Compassion Ministry through Food

For the *Real Life Prepper*, mercy and compassion may be a vital part of their life and it too requires some preparation. Even if the schumer has not hit the fan, a freak winter storm may drive someone who is hungry to your doorstep. Once again, Costco or Sam's may be able to help you out.

The *Real Life Prepper* does not have to prepare a sit down, pot roast dinner to demonstrate mercy and compassion. Sometimes a hot meal and support is just the ticket. RLP did not go through the process as a college student but heard many stories about folks who subsisted on noodles during tight financial times. RLP recognizes the value of a full stomach and is always willing to leverage what someone else already knows. One of the good things about Costco and Sam's is that you can put a case of anything in your cart and folks will hardly notice. RLP highly recommends you purchase a case or two of Ramen type noodles [L135] http://www.maruchan.com/ that already come in a serving bowl. They are cheap and are generally well accepted. In addition to the noodle bowls, you may want to investigate a case of self-contained plastic cutlery kits. The Boardwalk cutlery kit [L136] http://www.globalindustrial.com/ contains a disposable plastic knife, fork, spoon, napkin, salt, and pepper in an individually wrapped set. They are available everywhere. Through just the effort of making some hot water, you can meet someone's immediate needs quickly and cheaply. Cleanup afterwards is as easy as preparation. Besides, you never know when your brother-in-law is going to show up for that pot roast.

Plastic Sheeting for Windows and Doors

Shortly after the 9-11 terrorist attacks, the government decided to react. They made the very astute observation that we could be vulnerable in our own homes if the terrorists deployed a weapon that spread contamination across a broad area and that contamination made its way into our homes. It is simple enough to seal up the edges of our doors and windows with duct tape and plastic sheeting to help mitigate that risk. For the *Real Life Prepper*, that same solution may even keep their floor dry after a tornado or hurricane breaks a window pane. RLP highly recommends you purchase a couple rolls of at least 4-mil plastic sheeting and decent duct tape to use in an emergency. The plastic rolls come in both clear (transparent) and in black.

Pocket Knives

Back in the day, many folks carried a knife around in their pants pocket. My own father was famous for breaking out his Swiss Army knife and using the well worn scissors on a moment's notice. Today, we are afraid of our own shadows. Employees entering a federal office building where RLP used to work are still prohibited from bringing a Swiss Army knife into the building if it has a blade of any length. However, it there is an office birthday celebration occurring, you are allowed to bring in a very large and sharp knife to slice the cake with no questions asked.

RLP highly recommends the *Real Life Prepper* (male or female) purchase and get used to carrying a knife called an Every Day Carry (EDC). MrsRLP's EDC knife handle is bright yellow so she can easily find it in her purse. Your EDC knife should be able to be opened with only one hand. These types of knives normally use a thumb stud and are spring assisted to open. RLP highly recommends the type of knife represented by SOG [L142] www.sogknives.com called the Flash II. In addition to the thumb stud assist, it also has a safety lock that prevents it from opening inadvertently in your purse or pocket (something that is not expected anyway). Be aware that our government can and does make rules that interfere with our freedoms. Check out KnifeUp.com [L144] http://www.knifeup.com/knife-laws/ for guidance on state knife laws.

Sharpeners

The *Real Life Prepper* does not have to become an expert in knife sharpening. However, for proper preparation, you should consider having at least some sharpening tools available. A good place to start is a handheld manual sharpener. RLP highly recommends the Smith's PP1 Pocket Pal Multifunction Sharpener that sells for around $10. They are small enough and cheap enough to purchase several and distribute them as necessary. They make great Christmas stocking stuffers.

Sewing Kit

RLP does not sew on a routine basis. However, I am smart enough to realize the value of a small portable sewing kit. Do your own research as they are inexpensive and many are cheap. RLP recommends you purchase a small sewing kit that is packaged in a soft, zippered pouch of some type. After you figure out what makes sense for you, either choose another or modify the one you have to meet your needs. For instance, many come with multi-colored thread material. You may want to replace that with more muted thread. RLP specifically recommends against a hard case or one that does not zipper closed.

Funnels

Funnels are one of man's great inventions. Although you can make your own out of cardboard or paper, there is no substitute for a good, real funnel. RLP recommends you purchase several in different sizes and materials. Even stiff, plastic funnels can make your life easier. Consider them disposable. RLP also recommends you label the funnels as to use and not inadvertently contaminate the materials you are trying to handle. For fuel and oil transfer, nothing beats a metal funnel with a flexible spout.

Time

Modern man lives by the calendar and the clock. RLP loves his large digital display alarm clock with a battery backup. But batteries fail sometimes coincidentally with a temporary power outage. White tail deer do not care about failed batteries and have been known to walk through the woods while RLP was still asleep. RLP recommends the *Real Life Prepper* invest in an old fashioned key-wound alarm clock. Managing time can add some needed civility and order to your family even in normal circumstances.

Pets

The *Real Life Prepper* thinks about family pets as well as people during a crisis. They are relying on us to provide adequate care. In addition, they may return comfort or even security when we might be vulnerable. RLP recommends you store some dry pet food in a similar fashion as you store human food. This means oxygen absorbers, Mylar bags, food grade buckets, etc. Think about how you are going to continue management of an aquarium, particularly a salt water aquarium if you do not have power available.

Flea Prevention

The *Real Life Prepper* never knows when the zombie apocalypse is going to interrupt their supply of flea shampoo. Actually, MrsRLP prefers this recipe since it is more of a natural flea killer. These types of ingredients are real, everyday supplies you might already have on hand.

- 3 ounces liquid glycerin
- 3 ounces liquid Joy dish detergent
- 1 and ½ ounce white vinegar
- Fill the rest of the container with enough water to make 1 quart of shampoo.
- The RLP family dog seems to react to this flea shampoo better than harsh chemicals.

Entertainment

The *Real Life Prepper* should be prepared for entertainment options if the normal entertainment venues are not available. This applies to both adults and children. When you have an interruption in your normal routine, you do not want to give up. The *Real Life Prepper* not only survives, but thrives. Here are some ideas you can use to provide self-entertainment and a sense that civilization will continue.

- Books

- Board games
- Card games
- A *Real Life Prepper* may be looking for some cheap entertainment with Play Dough. In fact, it may be fun just to make it together.
  - 1 cup flour
  - ½ cup salt
  - 1 teaspoon cream of tartar
  - 1 Tablespoon oil
  - 1 cup colored water
  - Mix dry ingredients and oil. Add boiling water. Stir by hand or use a mixer until the mixer cleans the bowl (looks like a lumpy mess, and then all of a sudden, it looks great). Knead on a floured board. The Play Dough is hot, so you may find it easier to do this while wearing dish gloves. This also helps keep your hands from being stained by the food coloring while it works into the hot dough. Wilton food colors yield the brightest and best colors. Best stored in a Ziploc bag.

TRAINING AND SKILLS

One of RLP's passions is learning. That is one of the reasons I became a NRA instructor. In the prepper world, there is a saying that goes, "Knowledge is weightless." A backpack full of MREs, tactical gear, and a wheat grinder can get heavy. Somebody might steal your MREs or you may drop your tactical folder, but it will be hard to lose your first aid or pistol skills and they are not hard to carry. Of course there is even a Knowledge Weighs Nothing website [L106] http://knowledgeweighsnothing.com/

Many of the training opportunities presented here are as useful for the *Real Life Prep*per and everyday life as they are for the *Doomsday Prepper* and the zombie apocalypse. The *Real Life Prepper* may want to do an intentional analysis of skills and training needed before expending limited resources. RLP developed a Skills Matrix [A012] for the RLP family to assess our skill level, felt needs, and plans. Develop your own matrix based on the state of your own family. Existing skills are rated on a numerical scale with 5 being the highest. Even with a 5-rated skill, improvements can be made.

The NRA provides the best overall security training at the best overall value for the *Real Life Prepper*. This is not *Doomsday Prepper* stuff but every day, regular life stuff. You owe it to your family to check them out at the signup site [L021] **http://www.nrainstructors.org/searchcourse.aspx**. Refuse to be a Victim (RTBAV) is the course that RLP recommends the most. Suitable for most ages, it is a non-firearms course that helps your mindset in refusing to become a victim.

Appleseed [L022]

http://www.appleseedinfo.org/ provides great and inexpensive rifle marksmanship training associated with an appreciation of the U.S. Revolutionary War.

The Red Cross offers a variety of first aid, CPR, AED, and blood pathogen courses [L107] http://www.redcross.org/take-a-class.

The American Radio Relay League (ARRL) offers a variety of courses [L108] http://www.arrl.org/courses-training that help get your communication skills up to speed. There are plenty of internet based courses such as QSL.net [L109] http://www.qsl.net/aa0ni/toc.html/ that will help you get your HAM Technician license.

Definitely not just in the *Doomsday Prepper* world, Front Sight [L111] http://www.frontsight.com/ offers what RLP believes is the finest firearms training in the world for the *Real Life Prepper*. These courses are very highly recommended.

Sample Course Catalog
NRA Refuse To Be A Victim® Seminars

- Teaches the basic knowledge, skills, and attitude for developing a strategy for one's personal safety.
- The seminar includes classroom instruction on a variety of crime prevention strategies, from criminal psychology to automobile crimes to cyber crime. Seminars can vary in length, and may be modified to suit the needs of a particular audience. This is not a firearms instruction course, and does not include instruction in physical combat self-defense. Seminars teach about common weaknesses that criminals may take advantage of, and teaches a variety of corrective measures that are practical, inexpensive, and easy to follow. Strategies include home security, carjack avoidance

techniques, cyber safety, and use of personal safety devices. A complete seminar may last as long as eight hours and include the entire lesson plan, but a modified seminar may be as short as 90 minutes and address a specific topic. Students will receive the Refuse To Be A Victim student handbook, NRA Refuse To Be A Victim® brochure, NRA Become A Refuse To Be A Victim® Instructor Brochure, Refuse To Be A Victim® Firearms Supplement, and a course completion certificate.

NRA Home Firearm Safety Course

- Non-shooting course and teaches students the basic knowledge, skills, and to explain the attitude necessary for the safe handling and storage of firearms and ammunition in the home.
- This is a four-hour course for safe gun handling that is conducted in the classroom only. Students are taught NRA's three rules for safe gun handling; primary causes of firearms accidents; firearm parts; how to unload certain action types; ammunition components; cleaning; care; safe storage of firearms in the home; and the benefits of becoming an active participant in the shooting sports. Students will receive the NRA Home Firearm Safety handbook, NRA Gun Safety Rules brochure, Basic Firearm Training Program brochure, course completion certificate.

NRA FIRST Steps Pistol Orientation

- Firearm Instruction, Responsibility, and Safety Training — are the NRA's response to the American public's need for a firearm orientation program for new purchasers.
- NRA FIRST Steps Pistol is designed to provide a hands-on introduction to the safe handling and proper orientation to one specific pistol action type for classes of four or fewer students. This course is at least three hours long and includes classroom and range time learning to shoot a

specific pistol action type. Students will learn the NRA's rules for safe gun handling; the particular pistol model parts and operation; ammunition; shooting fundamentals; cleaning the pistol; and continued opportunities for skill development. Students will receive the Basics of Pistol Shooting handbook, NRA Gun Safety Rules brochure, Winchester/NRA Marksmanship Qualification booklet, FIRST Steps Course completion certificate.

NRA Basic Pistol Shooting Course

- Teaches the basic knowledge, skills, and attitude for owning and operating a pistol safely.
- This course is at least 8-hours long and includes classroom and range time learning to shoot revolvers and semi-automatic pistols. Students learn NRA's rules for safe gun handling; pistol parts and operation; ammunition; shooting fundamentals; range rules; shooting from the bench rest position, and two handed standing positions; cleaning the pistol; and continued opportunities for skill development. Students will receive the NRA Guide to the Basics of Pistol Shooting handbook, NRA Gun Safety Rules brochure, Winchester/NRA Marksmanship Qualification booklet, take a Basics of Pistol Shooting Student Examination, and course completion certificate.

NRA Defensive Pistol

- In Development

NRA FIRST Steps Rifle Orientation

- Firearm Instruction, Responsibility, and Safety Training — are the NRA's response to the American public's need for a firearm orientation program for new purchasers.
- NRA FIRST Steps Rifle is designed to provide a hands-on introduction to the safe handling and proper orientation to one specific rifle action type for classes of four or fewer students. This

course is at least three hours long and includes classroom and range time learning to shoot a specific rifle action type. Students will learn the NRA's rules for safe gun handling; the particular rifle model parts and operation; ammunition; shooting fundamentals; cleaning the rifle; and continued opportunities for skill development. Students will receive the Basics of Rifle Shooting handbook, NRA Gun Safety Rules brochure, Winchester/NRA Marksmanship Qualification booklet, FIRST Steps Course completion certificate.

NRA Basic Rifle Shooting Course

- Teaches the basic knowledge, skills, and attitude necessary for the safe use of a rifle in target shooting.
- This course is at least 14 hours long and includes classroom and range time learning to shoot rifles. Students learn NRA's rules for safe gun handling; rifle parts and operation; ammunition; shooting fundamentals; range rules; shooting from the bench rest, prone, sitting, standing and kneeling positions; cleaning, and continued opportunities for skill development. Students will receive the Basics of Rifle Shooting handbook, NRA Gun Safety Rules brochure, Winchester/NRA Marksmanship Qualification booklet; take a Basics of Rifle Shooting Student Examination, and course completion certificate.

NRA FIRST Steps Shotgun Orientation

- Firearm Instruction, Responsibility, and Safety Training are the NRA's response to the American public's need for a firearm orientation program for new purchasers.
- NRA FIRST Steps Shotgun course is designed to provide a hands-on introduction to the safe handling and proper orientation to one specific shotgun model. This course is at least three hours long and includes classroom and range

time learning to shoot a specific model shotgun at a moving target. Students will learn the NRA's rules for safe gun handling; the particular shotgun model parts and operation; ammunition; shooting fundamentals; cleaning the shotgun; and continued opportunities for skill development. Students will receive the Basics of Shotgun Shooting handbook, NRA Gun Safety Rules brochure, Winchester/NRA Marksmanship Qualification booklet, FIRST Steps Course completion certificate.

NRA Basic Shotgun Shooting Course

- Teaches the basic knowledge, skills, and attitude for the safe and proper use of a shotgun in shooting a moving target.
- This course is at least ten-hours long and includes classroom and range time learning how to shoot shotguns at moving targets. Students learn NRA's rules for safe gun handling; shotgun parts and operation; shotgun shell components; shotgun shell malfunctions; shooting fundamentals; range rules; shooting at straight away and angled targets; cleaning; and continued opportunities for skill development. Students will receive the Basics of Shotgun Shooting handbook, NRA Gun Safety Rules brochure, Winchester/NRA Marksmanship Qualification booklet; take a Basics of Shotgun Shooting Student Examination, and course completion certificate.

NRA Basic Personal Protection In The Home Course

- Teaches the basic knowledge, skills, and attitude essential to the safe and efficient use of a handgun for protection of self and family, and to provide information on the law-abiding individual's right to self-defense
- This is an eight-hour course. Students should expect to shoot approximately 100 rounds of

ammunition. Students will learn basic defensive shooting skills, strategies for home safety and responding to a violent confrontation, firearms and the law, how to choose a handgun for self-defense, and continued opportunities for skill development. Students will receive the NRA Guide to the Basics of Personal Protection In The Home handbook, NRA Gun Safety Rules brochure, the Winchester/NRA Marksmanship Qualification booklet, and course completion certificate.

NRA Basic Personal Protection In The Home course is for law-abiding adult citizens, as defined by applicable federal, state, or local law, and experienced shooters (shooters able to show mastery of the basic skills of safe gun handling, shooting a group, zeroing the firearm, and cleaning the firearm) to maximize what can be learned from this course. Proof of shooting experience can be one of the following: NRA Basic Pistol Course Certificate, NRA FIRST Steps Course Certificate, NRA pistol competitive shooting qualification card, military DD 214 with pistol qualification, or passing the Pre-Course Assessment.

Personal Protection Outside The Home Course

- Comprehensive and intensive in its approach to equip the defensive shooting candidate with the skills needed to survive serious adversity.
- The course teaches students the knowledge, skills and attitude essential for avoiding dangerous confrontations and for the safe, effective and responsible use of a concealed pistol for self-defense outside the home. Students have the opportunity to attend this course using a quality strong side hip holster that covers the trigger, or a holster purse. From a review of safe firearms handling and proper mindset to presentation from concealment and

multiple shooting positions, this course contains the essential skills and techniques needed to prevail in a life-threatening situation.

- The NRA Personal Protection Outside the Home is divided into two levels (basic and advanced). Level one is a nine-hour course and offers the essential knowledge and skills that must be mastered in order to carry, store, and use a firearm safely and effectively for personal protection outside the home. Upon completion of level one, students may choose to attend level two, which is an additional five hours of range training and teaches advanced shooting skills. After the classroom portion, students should expect to spend several hours on the range and shoot approximately 100 rounds of ammunition during level one. Level two involves five additional hours on the range and approximately 115 rounds of ammunition. The ammunition requirements are minimum and may be exceeded. Students will receive the NRA Guide to the Basics of Personal Protection Outside The Home handbook, NRA Gun Safety Rules brochure and the appropriate course completion certificates(s), NRA Basic Personal Protection Outside The Home (identifies strong-side hip holster or purse use) certificate, and NRA Advanced Personal Protection Outside The Home certificate.

- The NRA Basics of Personal Protection Outside The Home is for adult individuals who are not disqualified from possessing a firearm as defined by applicable federal, state, or local law and are of good repute and possess defensive pistol skills presented in the NRA Basics of Personal Protection In The Home Course. Participants must also understand the basic legal concepts relating to the use of firearms in self-defense, and must know and observe not only general gun safety rules, but also those safety principles that are specific to defensive situations. Prospective participants can demonstrate that they have the requisite knowledge, skills, and attitudes by producing an NRA Basic Personal Protection In The Home Course Certificate, or by passing the pre-course evaluation.

- Note: The Lesson III of the Personal Protection In and Outside The Home courses Firearms and the Law, and Legal Aspects of Self-Defense is conducted by an attorney licensed to practice law within the state in which this course is given and who is familiar with this area of the law, a Law Enforcement Officer (LEO) who possesses an intermediate or higher Peace Officer Standards and Training (POST) certificate granted within the state, or an individual currently certified to instruct in this area of the law by the state in which this course is presented.

NRA Basic Metallic Cartridge Reloading Course

- Teaches beginning reloaders the basic knowledge, skills, and attitude necessary to safely reload metallic cartridges.
- This course is eight hours in length and is conducted in a classroom. Each student is taught reloading safety; center fire cartridge components; using the reloading manual and reloading data; equipment; and the metallic cartridge reloading process. Students will receive the NRA Guide to Reloading handbook, the Basic Reloading Student Exam, a course completion certificate, NRA Gun Safety Rules brochure, a Basic Firearm Training Program brochure, and an Instructor Application/Course Evaluation form.

NRA Basic Shotgun Shell Reloading Course

- Teaches beginning reloaders the basic knowledge, skills, and attitude necessary to safely reload shotgun shells.
- This course is six hours in length and is conducted in a classroom. Each student is taught reloading safety; shotgun shell components; using the reloading manual and reloading data; equipment; and the shotgun shell reloading process. Students will receive the NRA Guide to Reloading handbook, the Basic Reloading Student Exam, a course completion certificate, NRA Gun Safety Rules brochure, a Basic Firearm Training Program brochure, and an Instructor Application Course/Evaluation form.

Energy Training

- General energy training
- We all understand how critical energy is to our civilization. RLP recently found a fairly inexpensive (read that as free) way to increase your knowledge about energy. Start out with the course "Fundamentals of Power" and work your way through batteries and generators. There are more than 200 web based courses available. Here is a friendly link that will take you to the Schneider Electric (APC) site [L110] http://www.myenergyuniversity.com.
- If you register, you can find out information about power, energy, racks, efficiency, and etc. courses. There is also information regarding an industry certification called Professional Energy Manager (PEM). If you are involved in electricity in any way (pretend you have electricity in your house), it might be to your advantage to at least take a few courses.
- You will need Adobe Flash Player and Adobe Shockwave installed to do the courses. You may have to use Google Chrome as your browser if you have other browser restrictions.

First Aid, CPR and AED Certification

- Red Cross Training
- Red Cross First Aid, CPR (cardiopulmonary resuscitation) and AED (automated external defibrillator) training and certification meets the needs of workplace responders, professional rescuers, school staffs, professional responders and healthcare providers, as well as the general public. They offer both certified and non-certified training options.

HAM Technician License

- First HAM License (QSL.net)
- This online course is meant for you to study for your first amateur radio license. Each lesson is followed by some review questions that you can print out and do by hand. Nothing on this site is copyrighted, so you're welcome to do whatever you like with it.

Front Sight

- Front Sight Training
- Attend a self-defense gun training course at Front Sight Firearms Training Institute's world-class firearms training facilities near Las Vegas, Nevada -- taught by seasoned and professional law enforcement, military, and private citizen instructors to levels that far exceed law enforcement and military standards, without any boot camp mentality or drill instructors attitudes. After your first self-defense firearms training course at Front Sight you will leave with self-defense firearms training skills that surpass 99% of the gun owning population! This is no exaggeration. Once you've completed your first Front Sight course you'll discover that you've become a self-defense gun training expert among your peers!

GLOSSARY AND ABBREVIATIONS

ARRL = American Radio Relay League – a national member association of amateur radio enthusiasts.

BATFE = Sometimes considered the nemesis to American liberty. The Bureau of Alcohol, Tobacco, Firearms, and Explosives. They regulate those commodities in the US. They can and will send you to jail, so be careful with their regulations.

BOB = Bug Out Bag – A bag, usually a pack, with preparation items pre-packed. You can throw your BOB on your back and get out of town.

BOL = Bug Out Location – An alternative safe location that you move to when the schumer hits the fan.

BOV = Bug Out Vehicle – a transportation mechanism a prepper uses to get out of the trouble area. In *Doomsday Preppers*, it is usually depicted as a Humvee (HMMWV) or a surplus Deuce-and-a-half. For a *Real Life Prepper*, it may be the family car, truck, motorcycle, boat, bicycle, or horse.

CFL = Compact Fluorescent Light Bulb – the curly light bulb that screws into your regular lamp and is supposed to save energy. It can be very dangerous.

CNG = Compressed Natural Gas

COLA = Cost of Living Adjustment – A fictitious number, generated by the U.S. government, that determines salary, benefit, and retirement increases.

CPR = Cardiopulmonary Resuscitation

CTCSS = Continuous Tone-Coded Squelch System – primarily used with walkie-talkies, a system used to segregate conversations using the same channel. It gives an illusion of privacy.

DCS = Digital Coded Squelch - primarily used with walkie-talkies, a system used to segregate conversations using the same channel. It gives an illusion of privacy.

EDC = Every Day Carry – Usually applies to a knife or firearm that you carry on a daily basis.

EMP = Electromagnetic Pulse – usually associated with an attack or a sunspot. An event causing disruption to electrical and electronic equipment.

EMT = Emergency Medical Technician

EPA = Environmental Protection Agency

FCC = Federal Communications Commission

FRN (1) = Federal Communications Commission Registration Number

FRN (2) = Federal Reserve Note – An IOU from the citizens of the United States to the Federal Reserve Bank. A substitute for real money.

FRS = Family Radio Service

GHB = Get Home Bag – Similar to the BOB. A bag, usually a pack, that you can use to get home from work or from wherever your car broke down.

GMO = Genetically Modified Organism

GMRS = General Mobile Radio Service

GPG = GNU Privacy Guard or GnuPG – A GPL Licensed alternative to the PGP suite. Should be free if you follow the rules.

ICE = In Case of Emergency – A person that you want

someone to contact if you are in trouble and someone is trying to help you. Generally an entry in your smart phone contacts list.

IWB = Inside the Waist Band – A holster designed to hang on your belt but on the inside of your pants. An IWB holster is usually easier to conceal than an OWB holster.

LEO = Law Enforcement Officer (usually a policeman or Sheriff).

LNG = Liquid Natural Gas

LPG = Liquid Petroleum Gas – otherwise known as Propane

MAG = Mutual Assistance Group – A group of like-minded people with some sort of common goal, usually support, in mind. A MAG can be compared to a MIG on steroids.

MIG = Mutual Interest Group - A group of like-minded people with some sort of common interest, usually educational, in mind.

MRE = Meals Ready to Eat. Other definitions are available from military personnel who have had to subsist on MREs.

MrsRLP = Mrs. Real Life Prepper – That mystical feminine partner of Real Life Prepper (RLP)

NRA = National Rifle Association – Probably the most well-known defender of our 2nd Amendment rights.

NREMT = Nationally Registered Emergency Medical Technician

OP AREA = Operational Area – This is where you work, live, play, and worship. Think of it as your stomping grounds. Your OP AREA includes your home, your neighborhood, where you shop, and the routes you take to get from one location to another.

OP SEC = Operational Security – This is fundamentally physical security of your home and operational area. Loose lips sink ships. OP SEC can be partially maintained by keeping your mouth shut. Do not tell untrusted folks how much food you have stored and do not post pictures of your machine gun on Facebook.

OWB = Outside the Waist Band – A holster designed to hang on your belt but on the outside of your pants.

PER SEC = Personal Security – This is your own personal security. You can help maintain your personal security by being aware of your surroundings and listening to your sixth sense.

PGP = Pretty Good Privacy – An encryption program, previously free, now available commercially.

PREPPER = Someone who is in some stage of coming to their senses. They are preparing for surviving, and even thriving when a disaster occurs. This disaster could be something like loss of a job, a flat tire, or the zombie apocalypse.

PTT = Push to talk – a button you use to transmit on a radio.

RLP = Real Life Prepper – The author of the book by the same name.

RTBAV = Refuse to be a Victim – A course offered by the NRA.

SCD (1) = Sub caliber device – Usually inserted into a flare gun to fire projectiles. May be regulated by the BATFE.

SCD (2) = Second Call Defense – An insurance and education organization designed to protect you in case of a firearm defense issue.

SCHUMER = A popular euphemism among preppers to keep from offending more sensitive ears. It is the digestive byproduct coming out of the south end of a north bound mule.

TACTICOOL = A play on the term tactical. Mall ninjas like to acquire gear that is tacticool. It looks tactical but the usefulness may be in question particularly if the holder has no training or the item has much more show than go. Putting an Airsoft scope on an AR-15 may look tactical but will probably fail when the AR-15 is fired. Many items are marketed in black just to make them look tactical. They are tacticool. Actually RLP has a black tactical clipboard.

UHF = Ultra-high frequency – a band of frequencies used for communications.

ULS = Federal Communications Commission Universal Licensing System – used to apply for a FCC license or to look up someone who has a license.

UPS = No, not the delivery company with the brown trucks. An uninterruptible power supply that converts DC battery power to the normally expected AC power used in your house.

VOX = Voice activated transmission – Usually associated with hands free operation of a radio where the sound of the voice activates the transmission. No PTT is necessary with VOX.

ZA = FCC ULS radio service code for GMRS

A TALE OF TWO CITIES EXERCISE

You may find it useful as an individual, family, or small group to complete this exercise. It will help you think about real life preparation without all of the doom and gloom associated with an end-of-the-world-as-we-know-it event. This exercise worksheet [A001] is available for electronic download at [L001] http://www.reallifeprepper.com

1. List the obvious, and not so obvious, things that Sherry did wrong in preparing for possible events.

2. What things did Sherry do right?

3. In the unprepared state she is in, what could Sherry have done to make things better?

4. If you are Sherry and got home safely, prioritize the top five (5) things you would do to prepare.

5. List the obvious things that Pepper did wrong in preparing for possible events.

6. What things did Pepper do right?

7. In the prepared state she is in, what could Pepper have done to make things better?

8. If you are Pepper and got home safely, prioritize the top five (5) things you would do to better prepare.

9. Why do you consider this a useful exercise?

A TALE OF TWO CITIES ANSWERS
Just One Man's Opinion

The exercise electronic worksheet answers are available for download at [L001] http://www.reallifeprepper.com

1. **List the obvious, and not so obvious, things that Sherry did wrong in preparing for possible events.**
- No battery backup for alarm clock
- Low gas in car
- Low food supply in pantry
- No available flashlights
- Does not check on family members before leaving
- Does not know how to operate garage door
- Does not lock up house when leaving
- Leaves briefcase in sight in car
- Only has a light sweater
- Walks on road in same direction as traffic
- No walking shoes available
- Knows only one way to get home
- Does not know how to treat water blister
- No first aid kit
- Drinks unclean water
- Looks and acts like a victim in public
- Allows strangers to know exactly where she lives

2. **What things did Sherry do right?**
- Brushes her teeth
- Uses a list for shopping

3. **In the unprepared state she is in, what could Sherry have done to make things better?**

4. **If you are Sherry and got home safely, prioritize the top five (5) things you would do to prepare.**

5. List the obvious things that Pepper did wrong in preparing for possible events.

- Some folks recommend locking bedroom door at night
- Did not try out radio until needed
- No written checklist for trip under duress
- Does not lock up house when leaving
- No hard copy list of contacts and customers

6. What things did Pepper do right?

- Backup battery for alarm clock
- Automatic light for power failure
- UPS for computer with automatic shutdown
- Assesses situation before leaving safety of bedroom
- Locks bedroom door when her gut tells her to
- Knows house well enough to get around in dark
- Knows sounds house makes
- Checks on family members before leaving
- If its yellow, let it mellow, if its brown, flush it down – saves water
- Has backup radio that needs no batteries
- Does not put faith in government
- Consults with family members
- Makes sure neighbors are okay – community
- Uses mental checklist
- Brings extra water for trip
- Has GHB in car
- Has hard copy road map in car
- Has first aid kit in car
- Has flashlight in car
- Knows how to operate garage door
- Enters dark business as a group
- Makes sign for customers at store
- Elects not to go through bad areas of town in crisis
- Knows how to use GPS to get alternative route
- Knows how to change flat tire
- Puts valuables in trunk of car
- Plans long walk before proceeding
- Leaves note in car for searchers

- Has working clothes in GHB
- Wears hat for protection

7. **In the prepared state she is in, what could Pepper have done to make things better?**

8. **If you are Pepper and got home safely, prioritize the top five (5) things you would do to better prepare.**

9. **Why do you consider this a useful exercise?**

EMERGENCY PROCEDURES AND INFORMATION
Updated October 5, 2011

Attorney Information
We have no "family" attorney nor do we pay any retainer for an attorney. However, in the case involving firearms, we do have a contact attorney. RLP met this attorney when he attended the NRA Personal Defense in the Home course.

Firearms Attorney: Jack Wolverine, partner at Dewey, Cheatham and Howell.

Bug Out Information
Remember the pass phrase. If someone - including a stranger - uses the pass phrase and asks you to do something, it means your spouse trusted them enough and you probably should follow their instructions.

You must prioritize what you bug out with. You cannot take everything. We have a blue bug-out-box (BOB) trunk with wheels. Take the BOB along with the critical document folder from the large gun safe. Then take both emergency packs and Wiggy's sleeping bags. Take the gold, silver, the firearms, and the ammunition. Shutdown the computer, then disconnect and take the designated external hard drive.

Our default meeting location (if we have to evacuate) is our home. Walk home if necessary and consider the way through the park if the situation warrants it. If the home is not accessible, meet at the church. If the church is not accessible, meet at the Lowes at the corner of I-22 and Summer Street.

Communications Plan

The RLP family will standardize on the Midland GXT1050 walkie-talkies. Normally we will communicate with each other using channel 17 and digital coded squelch (DCS) 17. In case there are issues, shift to channel 22 with DCS 22 for thirty minutes. Until communications are reestablished, keep trying 17 and 17 every thirty minutes at 15 minutes past and 15 minutes before the hour.

In an emergency situation, attempt regular contact at 15 minutes past the hour. Keep these communications short.

It is important that we all maintain charged cell phones if possible. On a normal basis, use texting. Call if necessary. Charge your phone when the opportunity arises.

If voice or texting communications become unavailable, we still need to keep in contact. If you must leave home, leave a written message on the kitchen bulletin board that clearly communicates your intentions.

Firearms Incident

Your memory can fool you. Our policy is that we do not share the details of the incident with **anyone** outside of our spouse and attorney. The only thing you should share with either the 911 dispatcher or the police is that you were in fear for your – or someone's – life, you shot until you stopped them, and then you want to talk to your attorney.

First Aid and Medical Information

The large, "ready" medical kit is on the shelf above the doorway in the master bedroom closet. It is a red, transparent plastic box with a clear plastic lid. The trauma first aid kit is in a bright (orange) shoulder bag. The trauma kit is usually kept with or in the range bag. Both of these kits have wound blood clotting materials, usually Celox.

The large, off-the-shelf first aid kit is in the blue bug-out-box.

Doctor: Dr. Blood Stopper 863-555-1212

Dentist: Dr. Pain Stopper   863-666-2323

Hazardous Materials
Ammunition
Ammunition can be stored anywhere in the house. Firearms in the safe rooms are loaded and ready to use. Bulk ammunition is stored together. Currently there is a large cache in the closet between the master bath and laundry room. There is bulk ammunition in the long term storage area. There may be ammunition in the night stand and in the reloading bench.

Gasoline
Gasoline is any large quantity is stored outside in the plastic shed under the screen porch.

Gun Powder
We have a quantity of smokeless gun powder in one (1) pound and eight (8) pound containers. It is stored safely in the reloading bench in the same part of the basement with the large gun safe. Although not explosive, it does burn rapidly and should be kept separate from primers, gasoline, or other flammable materials.

Kerosene
We have some kerosene stored in both plastic 2-gallon containers and metal 5-gallon drums. Kerosene is

flammable and should be treated with caution.

Paint

We have both spray cans and liquid cans of paint stored in the garage on the shelf next to the front wall.

Primers

Primers are inherently dangerous and are explosive. They should be kept in their original containers. They are stored in a separate (right) section of the reloading bench.

Propane

Propane in any large quantity is stored outside in the plastic shed under the screen porch.

Police Contact Incident

Our policy is that we do not allow any searches of our vehicles, our homes and near structures, nor our persons without demonstration of probable cause or a search warrant. This applies whether or not we feel the police contact is friendly.

Safe Information

There are two built-in safes in the house. The one in the upstairs safe room requires batteries. The other one has a mechanical lock. The two locks have the same combination.

There is one large "gun" safe in the basement. It has a mechanical lock. This safe has a manufacturer-supplied combination that cannot be changed.

Utility Information and Shutdown
Electrical

All electrical power from the street enters the house near the meter, midway down the length of the

driveway, on the house side of the driveway. The
electrical power cable is buried underground, comes up
through the concrete driveway, through the meter, and
elbows into the garage. There is only one power
distribution panel so all power inside of the house can be
cut off by using the uppermost main breaker. Tripping
the main breaker does not entirely remove power from
the panel because the upstream side of the main breaker
is still hot. The power meter must be disconnected to
remove electrical power completely from the
distribution panel.

Natural Gas

All natural gas enters the house through an
above-ground gas meter on the west-end (opposite the
driveway side) of the house. The non-metal gas line
supplying the meter is buried underground and comes
from the street. A metal wire is wrapped around the non-
metal line so that the line can be found with a metal
detector. The gas to the house can be cut off using the
valve on the top of the meter itself. The valve is operated
using the metal emergency tool. The red emergency tool
is hanging on a nail on the door frame just inside the
people door on the north-west corner of the garage. The
tool can also be used to shut-off the water main. An
alternative tool is the silver looking On Duty 4-in-1
Emergency Tool hanging right next to it.

Copper gas supply lines inside the house run in
the overhead of the garage. They are labeled "GAS" and
have individual, manually-operated shut-off valves in
each line supplying each gas-operated appliance. When
the valve handle is in line with the copper line, the gas is
on and the gas can flow to the appliance. To turn the gas
off to an individual appliance, turn the handle 90 degrees
or perpendicular to the gas line. The gas fireplace logs
have an additional gas shutoff valve inside the fire box

on the bottom right side. Here the appliances.

- Gas oven (kitchen)
- Gas range (kitchen)
- Gas fireplace logs (living room)
- Gas furnace for main living area (in garage)
- Gas furnace for master bedroom (in garage)
- Gas furnace for second floor (in attic)

Water

The water meter is underground under a rectangular metal cover that is just below the surface level of the lawn. The meter is to the side of the driveway at the top of the hill and on the opposite side from the house. The emergency tool, hanging on a nail on the door frame just inside the people door on the north-west corner of the garage, can be used to shut off either the water main and/or the gas meter.

Lawn Sprinkler

The control system is right next to the power distribution box in the garage. It receives its power from a transformer that is normally plugged into the outlet just below the distribution panel. Normally we leave the lawn sprinkler control box **door open** when the system is **on**. There are four zones and three cycle schedules. Normally we run the system manually or use cycle schedule A. The zones are:

- Zone 1 – the four (4) rotary spray heads on the front lawn
    - In the corner next to the mail box
    - In the adjacent corner next to the big power transformers hidden by the multiple Grey Owl junipers next to the street
    - Next to the curve of the sidewalk, midway between the driveway and front porch

- In the center of the garden area between
  the crepe myrtle and the Japanese maple
- Zone 2 – the three (3) spray heads evenly
  distributed along the sidewalk on the house side
- Zone 3 – the ten (10) spray heads evenly
  distributed along the edge of the house from the
  gas meter around to the end of the deck opposite
  the stairs.
- Zone 4 – the six (6) spray heads evenly
  distributed from where Zone 3 ends at the
  bottom of the driveway around the corner and
  up on the hillside next to the brick retaining wall
  on the side opposite the house. The last spray
  head is next to the water meter at the top of the
  driveway.

Telephone

The telephone line is buried underground. I
think, but am not sure, that the line comes from the area
near the large power transformers hidden by the multiple
Grey Owl junipers to the corner of the South-East corner
of the house where the electrical power and telephone
enter the house. The wire then runs into a utility box in
the garage next to the Lawn Sprinkler control box. The
utility box does not have a cover on it. The telephone
lines within the house all terminate in that box along
with the coaxial cable lines (used for satellite and cable).
You can change which existing telephone outlets in the
house are used by changing the jumpers in the utility
box.

Currently we only use three telephone
connections. One connection is in the kitchen. The base
station is plugged in there, through a DSL filter, and all
other remote telephones communicate through a wireless
connection to the base station. The second connection,
through a DSL filer, is behind the stereo equipment
cabinet and was used for the satellite receiver
connection. The third connection is in the middle

bedroom upstairs. It has no DSL filer and is used only
for the internet connection on the computer.

Internet
The internet connection is high-speed ADSL,
supplied by AT&T through the regular telephone lines.
Currently the only hard-wired internet connection is in
the middle bedroom upstairs. There is a wireless
connection available. The pass phrase, inscribed in
concrete at the church, refers to the Bible.

In November of 2010, we added an Ethernet
cable running from the box behind the computer in the
middle bedroom upstairs, down through the wall in to
the basement. The wire then runs in the basement ceiling
into the wall between the master bedroom and living
room. It is used to connect the Roku box to the internet.

Satellite TV
We used to have DISH. The satellite dish is on
the North-East corner of the roof, over the non-screened
in deck. The double cable runs down the exterior house
wall and into the garage. It runs in the garage ceiling
into the same utility box as the telephone connections.
There are pre-existing cable connections in the house.
They are reconfigured in the utility box.

Cable TV
No cable television. But, if we had a connection,
it would be into the utility box and distributed
throughout the house the same way as the satellite
television.

REAL LIFE PREPPER LIBRARY

Every proper prepper needs to have a library. The internet is fine, Kindle is good, but not much beats a hard copy when everything else fails. You will find you have a need for general information, reference material, ideas, general moral support, encouragement, and entertainment. RLP purposely did not list all possible library materials. The sample library materials are arranged in alphabetical order by logical categories into sections. Have fun and explore the possibilities. These are just suggestions that have proven useful in the past. They are designed to touch your palate and generate interest. For the *Doomsday Prepper*, this would be a prioritized list of library materials you have to have and it would look like a formal English garden. For the *Real Life Prepper*, this is more like a comfortable garden of ideas, seeded by the winds and experiences from past years. The Library section is split up into non-fiction and fiction materials. Sometimes it is not as easy as you would expect to differentiate between non-fiction and fiction. Where possible, reviews of materials or a synopsis are provided.

Non-Fiction

Skills, Communications Section

Ham Radio For Dummies

- Silver H. Ward
- It's time we cleared the air about ham radio. If you think of it as staticky transmissions sent by people in the middle of nowhere, think again. Today's ham radio goes beyond wireless to extreme wireless, Operators transmit data and

pictures, use the internet, laser, and microwave transmitters, and travel to places high and low to make contact. In an emergency or natural disaster, ham radio can replace downed traditional communication and save lives. Whether you're just getting turned on to ham radio or already have your license, *Ham Radio for Dummies* helps you with the terminology, the technology and the talknology. You discover how to:

- Decipher the jargon and speak the language
- Buy or upgrade your equipment, including the all-important antennas
- Build a ham radio shack, complete with the rig, a computer, mobile/base rig, microphones, keys, headphones, antennas, cables and feed lines
- Study for your license, master Morse code, take the test and get your call sign
- Understand the basics of ragchews (conversations), nets (organized on-air meetings) and DX-ing (competing in contacts to make contacts)
- Keep logs with the vital statistics, including time (in UTC or World Time), frequency, and call sign
- Written by an electrical engineer, Certified Amateur Radio License Examiner, and columnist for QST, a monthly magazine for ham operators, *Ham Radio for Dummies* gives you the info you need to delve into the science or dive into the conversation. It explains how you can:
- Tune in to the most common types of signals, including Morse Code (CW), single-sideband (SSB), FM, Radio teletype (RTTY), and data signals
- Break in, introduce yourself, converse, and say or signal goodbye
- Communicate while traveling (ham radio goes where mobile phones go dead)

- Register with an emergency organization such as ARES and RACES Help in emergencies such as earthquakes, wildfires, or severe weather
- Pursue your special interests, including contacting distant stations, participating in contests, exploring the digital modes, using satellites, transmitting images, and more
- Complete with a glossary and ten pages of additional suggested resources, *Ham Radio for Dummies* encourages you to touch that dial and take that mike
- CUL. (That's Morse Code for "see you later.")

Skills, Handyman Section

How To Weld

- Todd Bridigum
- Welding is a skill that any do-it-yourself enthusiast needs in his arsenal. It's only when you can join metal that you can properly repair and create. This book is the perfect introduction for neophytes and an excellent refresher for veteran welders, a work so comprehensive and so complete that most readers won't need any further instruction. How to Weld starts with a brief history of welding, an overview of the different types of welding, and a thorough discussion of safety practices. Longtime welding instructor Todd Bridigum describes various tools and types of metals, as well as techniques and types of joints. Bridigum discusses gas, stick, wire-feed (MIG and TIG), even brazing, completing each section with a series of exercises that fully illustrate the skills he has covered.

Machinery's Handbook 29th Edition

- Erik Oberg

- A reference book for the Mechanical Engineer, designer, manufacturing engineer, draftsman, toolmaker, and machinist. This is the book you need if you are going to reboot civilization from your basement after the zombie apocalypse. There is a toolbox edition (smaller print), a large print edition, and a combo edition that comes with a CD.

Machine Shop Essentials

- Frank Marlow
- Do you know what a Silver & Deming drill bit is? Do you know what type of drill bit to use for sheet metal? Do you know the difference between a number drill and letter drill? Do you know what type of hammer you are supposed to use on a chisel? Do you know how to select and use a file? If you want to keep me from cutting a corner off of your Man Card, you need to know these things. I am sending out a recommendation for two books that I wished I had owned at age 20. Although fairly pricey, they are worth the money. They make a great gift for a son or husband. Be careful; they may be useful for a woman that is so inclined but they both have testosterone literally dripping from them. Just owning them makes your biceps bigger, makes you attractive to women of all ages, and causes a little male pattern baldness. It took me two months to read them both. They are in a topic/question-and-answer format and all sections are not applicable to me. I learned a lot that I can immediately use and much of the rest I will use as reference material. They both take a machine shop perspective but much of the information transcends all aspects of being a handy man (or woman).
- If you get just one, try *Machine Shop Essentials* (the brown one). No, I did not pay $157. *Machine Shop Know-How* (the blue one) has less immediately useful information but it is still worthwhile.

- *Machine Shop Essentials: Questions & Answers* by Frank Marlow
- *Machine Shop Know-How: The Tips & Techniques of Master Machinists* by Frank Marlow

The Milling Machine for Home Machinists

- Harold Hall

Visual Guide to Lock Picking

- Mark McCloud
- The *Visual Guide to Lock Picking* discusses tubular locks, combination padlocks, and lever locks. What really sets this book apart is the quality of illustrations, which make lock picking easy to understand. The visual approach makes it easy to see how locks really work. Each type is completely dissected, exposing every moving part. Step-by-step instructions are given for picking each kind of lock. You will be led through the entire process, from introducing the necessary tools, to explaining several techniques that will lead you to that satisfying click as your lock springs open! This book is the premier guide on picking locks. Even if you already know how to pick some locks, this book covers tips and techniques. Exercises are also explained to help you hone your skills. From simple locks, to high security pins, almost all modern lock types are covered; making it the perfect locksmith's companion. Whether you are interested in becoming a locksmith, need to know how to bypass security locks for law enforcement or emergency services, interested in lock picking as a hobby, practicing for an upcoming competition, or just want to be prepared in an emergency, this book will get you started off right!

Skills, Health Care Section

Herbal Home Health Care

- John R. Christopher
- This is an excellent reference volume of natural health care for both children and adults. It lists diseases in convenient alphabetical order with concise definitions, symptom descriptions, causes and herbal aids. Other natural treatments are outlined, including the cold sheet treatment, the incurables program, detoxification and the mucus less diet. A book for every family.

Medicinal Wild Plants

- Steven Foster
- A Field Guide to Medicinal Plants is the first comprehensive, pocket-size guide to this engrossing subject. Not only does it tell how to identify 500 medicinal plants, it also describes in detail all the known uses- both folk remedies and those that have been scientifically proven.

Where There Is No Doctor

- David Werner
- More than just a first aid book
- Covers medical care when and where there is no Doctor available

Skills, Homemaking Section

A Guide To Canning, Freezing, Curing & Smoking Meat, Fish & Game

- Wilbur F. Eastman

- This no-nonsense guide to canning, freezing, curing, and smoking meat, fish, and game is written in down-to-earth, informative, everyday language. The third edition of this perennial bestseller is completely revised and updated to comply with the latest USDA health and safety guidelines. Includes dozens of delicious recipes for homemade Beef Jerky, Pemmican, Venison Mincemeat, Corned Beef, Gepockelete (German-style cured pork), Bacon, Canadian Bacon, Smoked Sausage, Liverwurst, Bologna, Pepperoni, Fish Chowder, Cured Turkey, and a variety of hams. Learn tasty pickling methods for tripe, fish, beef, pork, and oysters. An excellent resource for anyone who loves meat but hates the steroids and chemicals in commercially available products.

The Dehydrator Bible: Includes Over 400 Recipes

- Jennifer MacKenzie
- The comprehensive handbook for dehydrating foods at home. Dehydrating is one of the most effective ways to preserve food for maximum nutrition at very low cost. Sales of dehydrators are soaring as many cooks reject the suspect ingredients in commercially prepared foods. Dehydrating with the recipes in this book is one way to control all ingredients and please the whole family. Recipes for dried ingredients include herbs and seasonings, fruits, fruit leathers, vegetables and beef jerky. These nutritious ingredients are included in delicious recipes such as: Beef and potato stew, Chicken pot pie, Vegetable lasagna, Zucchini and red pepper fritters, Dried tomato and basil polenta Mushroom, herb and white wine sauce Strawberry rhubarb tarts. These recipes appeal to a wide array of tastes, feature contemporary ingredients such as whole grains and work equally well in a home kitchen, on an RV, on a boat or at a campsite. Recommendations for buying a dehydrator and storing dehydrated

foods are also included. Easy-to-follow instructions with specific time guidelines and best practices and the latest data on food safety make this the ideal dehydrating guidebook and cookbook.

Skills, Homesteading Section

New Complete Guide To Gardening

- Better Homes & Gardens
- An invaluable reference for both novice and experienced gardeners with 600 full-color pages packed with over 750 photos of overall gardens and individual plants. Readers will find complete information on perennials, roses, bulbs, annuals, lawns, trees, shrubs, vines, ground covers, fruits, vegetables, and herbs.270 pages of plant encyclopedias provide detailed how-to-grow-it information for nearly 500 plants. A photo accompanies each encyclopedia entry.100 page special design section helps homeowners translate basic information into specific solutions for the challenges in their own yard. Step-by-step illustrations show all the techniques critical to proper plant maintenance. Dozens of handy charts help readers at a glance learn which plants are best for which situations. Information provided for all regions of the country.

The Encyclopedia Of Country Living

- Carla Emery
- The most complete source of information available about growing, processing, cooking, and preserving homegrown foods from the garden or field. This revised and updated edition of the classic text is an indispensable resource on country living.

- Illustrated.

All New Square Foot Gardening

- Mel Bartholomew
- Do you know what the best feature is in "All New Square Foot Gardening"? Sure, there are ten new features in this all-new, updated book. Sure, it's even simpler than it was before. Of course, you don't have to worry about fertilizer or poor soil ever again because you'll be growing above the ground. But, the best feature is that "anyone," "anywhere" can enjoy a Square Foot garden. Children, adults with limited mobility, even complete novices can achieve spectacular results. But, let's get back to the ten improvements. You're going to love them. 1) New Location - Move your garden closer to your house by eliminating single-row gardening. Square Foot Garden needs just "twenty percent" of the space of a traditional garden. 2) New Direction - Locate your garden "on top" of existing soil. Forget about pH soil tests, double-digging (who enjoys that?), or the never-ending soil improvements. 3) New Soil - The new "Mel's Mix" is the perfect growing mix. Why, we even give you the recipe. Best of all, you can even "buy" the different types of compost needed. 4) New Depth - You only need to prepare a SFG box to a depth of 6 inches! It's true--the majority of plants develop just fine when grown at this depth. 5) No Fertilizer - The all new SFG does not need any fertilizer-ever! If you start with the perfect soil mix, then you don't need to add fertilizer. 6) New Boxes - The new method uses bottomless boxes placed aboveground. We show you how to build your own (with step-by-step photos). 7) New Aisles - The ideal gardening aisle width is about three to four feet. That makes it even easier to kneel, work and harvest. 8) New Grids - Prominent and permanent grids added to your SFG box help you visualize the planting squares and know

how to space for maximum harvest. 9) New Seed Saving Idea - The old-fashioned way advocates planting many seeds and then thinning the extras (that means pulling them up). The new method means planting a pinch- literally two or three seeds--per planting hole. 10) Tabletop Gardens - The new boxes are so much smaller and lighter (only 6 inches of soil, remember?), you can add a plywood bottom to make them portable. Of course, that's not all. We've also included simple, easy-to-follow instructions using lots of photos and illustrations. You're going to love it!

Skills, Security, Firearms Section

ABC's Of Reloading: The Definitive Guide For Novice To Expert

- Bill Chevalier

Barnes Reloading Manual 4

Boston's Gun Bible

- Boston T. Party
- A very good overview of why firearms are so critical to our liberty
- Provides specific recommendations for prioritizing purchases
- Combines the soul behind the tools of Liberty along with technical information

Building Your AR15 from Scratch

- A DVD, not a book, but even better.
- Both the announcer and the hands on builder/instructor speak very clearly and in English! The announcer/moderator sort of fills

the viewer's role as if it was a live class. When necessary, they zoom in very close (with sharp images) and you can see what is really going on. I highly recommend the DVD purchase even if you are not building but rather modifying or buying. They make specific recommendations and give you tips that can make a big difference. For instance, do you know there is a difference between the diameter of mil-spec and commercial stock extension? Just the descriptions of special tools alone are worth the cost of the DVD. But what do I know; I have only watched it three times and am working my way through the fourth. P.S. Use your pause button and take notes.

- Available from Amazon for about $20.

Firearms Guide

- Impressum Media
- DVD
- Specifications, Tech Specs, Diagrams of 57,000 Firearms and 4,300 schematics

Hornady Handbook of Cartridge Reloading

Lyman Reloading Handbook

Modern Reloading

- Richard Lee

Nosler Reloading Guide 6

Skills, Security, General Section

A Failure of Civility

- Mike Garand and Jack Lawson

- Provides very specific and practical guidance for organizing your own neighborhood for the zombie apocalypse.
- Could be scary for the *Real Life Prepper* but it will probably make you think in directions you have not yet explored.
- Recommended but not as your first exposure into prepping.
- Leans more to the *Doomsday Prepper* than the *Real Life Prepper*

Society Ending Events: The First 180 Days

- Bob Gaskin
- I briefly met Bob Gaskin during the September 2013 Oxford, AL Preparedness Seminar. He seemed like any other of the many guys thinking about survival and how to protect his family. Normal? No, but then again neither am I, nor am I looking for normal. My wife went to his training session and we bought a copy of his book, *Society Ending Events: The First 180 Days* that he autographed, "Eyes Open! No Fear!" His eleven chapter book has no page numbers which makes it less useful as a reference but the 120 or so pages make it readable in just a couple of sittings. There is a good combination of unanswered questions, sometimes in the form of scenarios, and recommended actions, sometimes in the form of lists. If you read *A Failure of Civility*, you will see a common theme. Keep your eyes open. Prepare. And if you try to survive by yourself, you will die. You need community. Bob has a stated mission. It may scare you to inaction. It may encourage you to open your eyes, pay attention, and take reasonable steps to protect your family. He says, "It is my personal belief, that by the end of 2016, this planet will go through a series of events that will bring about a Society Ending Event here in the United States. It is also my belief that less than 6% of us will

survive…." I found the section discussing the five stages of preparation particularly interesting. It caused me to reconsider what I am doing and where I want to go. This is not a must-have book, but it is a helpful book. I would not recommend it for someone who is just starting to think about preparations. But if you are willing to step back and think about what you are doing, it will help you gain some perspective.

Skills, Security, Privacy and Computers Section

PGP & GPG – Email for the Practical Paranoid

- Michael W. Lucas

Skills, Survival Section

Crisis Preparedness Handbook

- Jack A. Spigarelli
- A comprehensive guide to home storage and physical survival
- Lots of references and checklists
- Leans more to the *Real Life Prepper* than the *Doomsday Prepper*

How To Survive The End Of The World As We Know It: Tactics, Techniques, And Technologies For Uncertain Times

- James Wesley, Rawles
- The ultimate guide to total preparedness and self-reliance, this work, written by one of the best-known survival experts, contains

everything people need to know in order to
prepare and protect themselves.

Real Life Prepper

- RLP (alias Frank Cohee)
- The finest prepping book on the market. This
  should be your first purchase for your survival
  and prepping library. Packed with concrete
  recommendations, it is vastly entertaining.

SAS Survival Handbook

- John 'Lofty' Wiseman
- A reference book for hikers, campers, and
  outdoor adventurers
- A Boy Scout handbook on steroids

Strategic Relocation – North American Guide to Safe Places

- Joel M. Skousen
- Very interesting perspective on geographical
  considerations for safety. Get this one to see
  where you are as compared to the rest of the
  country and consider Skousen's safety factors.
- Not quite a coffee table book, but a good
  reference you will find yourself revisiting often.

Surviving Doomsday: A Guide for Surviving an Urban Disaster

- Richard Duarte
- A step by step guide to help you prepare to
  survive an urban disaster. A simple and easy-to-
  understand approach to help you plan for a
  potential crisis. Strategies to help you secure the
  core survival elements - food, water, first aid,
  security, and sanitation. Tips on when to stay
  put, and when to get out. Tactics to keep you
  and your family safe during a crisis.

- Extensive shopping lists for survival products and supplies.

Fiction

Expatriates: A Novel of the Coming Global Collapse

- James Wesley, Rawles
- Four of four in the series (2013)

Founders: A Novel of the Coming Collapse

- James Wesley, Rawles
- Three of four in the series (2012)

Lights Out

- David Crawford
- The first EMP novel RLP read. Set in Texas, it can be kind of scary but it is very entertaining.

Molon Labe

- Boston T. Party (alias Kenneth W. Royce)
- One of RLP's favorite novels, very much based in Libertarian ideas.

One Second After

- William R. Forstchen
- New York Times bestselling author William R. Forstchen now brings us a story which can be all too terrifyingly real...a story in which one man struggles to save his family and his small North Carolina town after America loses a war, in one second, a war that will send America back to the Dark Ages...A war based upon a weapon, an Electro Magnetic Pulse (EMP). A weapon that may already be in the hands of our enemies. Months before publication, *One Second After* has already been cited on the floor

of Congress as a book all Americans should read, a book already being discussed in the corridors of the Pentagon as a truly realistic look at a weapon and its awesome power to destroy the entire United States, literally within one second. It is a weapon that the Wall Street Journal warns could shatter America. In the tradition of *On the Beach, Fail Safe* and *Testament*, this book, set in a typical American town, is a dire warning of what might be our future...and our end.

Patriots: A Novel of Survival In The Coming Collapse

- James Wesley, Rawles
- Read this one first, One of four in the series (2009)
- Part novel, part survivalist-handbook, "Patriots" tells of a small group of friends facing every American's worst nightmare--the total collapse of society. The stock market plummets and hyperinflation cripples commerce and then a seemingly isolated financial crisis passes the tipping point when an unprepared government fails to act. Practically overnight, the fragile institutions of democracy fall apart and every American is forced to survive on their own. Evading mobs of desperate, out-of-control citizens who have turned Chicago into a wasteland of looting and mayhem, this novel's protagonists make their way to a shared secure ranch in the wilds of northern Idaho. Here the survival-driven group fends off vicious attacks from the outside and eventually assists in restoring order to the country. The compelling, fast-paced action-adventure novel has readers jotting notes and referencing the book's impressive index for informative survivalist tips on everything from setting up a secure shelter to treating traumatic flesh wounds.

Survivors: A Novel of the Coming Collapse

- James Wesley, Rawles
- Two of four in the series (2011)

ONLINE RESOURCES

The internet is full of information, some good and some bad. Here are some initial resources you can look at if the subject stimulates your interests.

American Preppers Network

- http://www.americanpreppersnetwork.net/
- The official forum of the American Preppers Network (APN)

Frugal's Squirrels

- http://www.frugalsquirrels.com/
- A forum of like-minded people helping each other to be prepared.

Prepper Groups

- http://www.preppergroups.com/
- It's time to meet, network, discuss!

Survivalblog

- http://www.survivalblog.com/
- or try the IP address 95.143.193.148
- The Daily Web Log for Prepared Individuals Living in Uncertain Times.

SAMPLE SIMPLIFIED INCOME PLAN

In essence, it is a simple breakdown of your monthly and annual income for the rest of your life. You probably know exactly how much money from what source you will make in January of 2013. You also know the same thing for October of 2015 (when you retire), for the month that you decide to start drawing social security, and what is going to be available for your family when they survive you (whenever that is).

If you can track projections, you can make plans to supplement, enhance, or mitigate risks. If you do not know what is going on, you cannot take any actions to make it better. What is the best option? Should you have $100,000 in the bank or should you have a "guaranteed" check come in at $5,000 every month for the rest of your life? In order to retire comfortably, you should expect to make about 70% to 80% of what you are living on comfortably while working. Do yourself and your family a favor and make your own plan. You will thank RLP later.

Here is an example of a SIP. This purposely does not factor in raises, COLA, taxes, expenses, or other assets like life insurance. Keep it simple.

Source	January 2013 (Today)	October 2015 (Retirement)	March 2017 (Start drawing SSA)	Upon Survival
Regular salary	$60,000	$12,000	$12,000	$6,000
SSA	$0	$0	$18,000	$9,000
Monthly	$5,000	$1,000	$2,500	$1,250
Annual	$60,000	$12,000	$30,000	$15,000

Can you both survive and thrive like this? Now you can start making plans to strengthen what you need to. For instance, should you look for advancement, a part-time job, or invest more in an IRA? What kind of life insurance do you need to provide for your survivors?

ABOUT THE AUTHOR

RLP, alias Frank Cohee, was raised an Army brat. His father gave him some good advice, "Join the Navy." RLP graduated from the U.S. Naval Academy with a BSAE and entered the Navy Nuclear Power program. After serving on two nuclear powered guided missile cruisers, RLP taught management courses at Georgia Tech where he earned a MSNE. RLP was a certified NREMT for a while. Leaving active duty, RLP worked for the civilian nuclear power industry cleaning up the damaged Three Mile Island nuclear reactor then as a Startup Test Engineer. RLP ran his own computer consulting business for a number of years and then went to work for the federal government. RLP earned a MBA from the University of Alabama in Birmingham. RLP retired from the Naval Reserve as a Captain, with three separate commands. After starting a Project Management Office for a software development firm, RLP went to work for the U.S. Treasury as an IT manager and recently retired. RLP's military certifications include: Navy Nuclear Engineer and Surface Warfare Officer. RLP earned more than a dozen information technology certifications plus the Project Management Institute PMP certification. RLP is a certified NRA firearms instructor and loves to teach. RLP is also an Elder in the PCA, a father of two, and a grandfather of three. He currently resides with MrsRLP in the Southeast.

www.ingramcontent.com/pod-product-compliance
Lightning Source LLC
Chambersburg PA
CBHW070800280326
41934CB00012B/2986